KOINS MOTEL

The Last Resort

D. O'BRIEN

Set in a seaside Resort Town on the Queensland Coast of Australia amid the glitz and glamour of a Millionaires playground, a tale of exploitation by the wealthy of the disenfranchised, the homeless, the pensioners and the labourers. Of drug dealers, thieves, addicts and street workers.

Based on a true story. Names have been changed to protect the innocent.

Published by D. O'Brien 2015

Copyright © 2015 D. O'Brien

All rights reserved. No part of this publication may be reproduced, stored in a retrieval system, or transmitted in any form or by any means, electronic, mechanical, photocopying, recording or otherwise, without the prior written permission from the publisher.

Disclaimer
Every effort has been made to ensure that this book is free from error or omissions. Information provided is of general nature only and should not be considered legal or financial advice. The intent is to offer a variety of information to the reader. However, the author, publisher, editor or their agents or representatives shall not accept responsibility for any loss or inconvenience caused to a person or organisation relying on this information.

A catalogue record for this book is available from the National Library of Australia.

Book cover design and formatting services by BookCoverCafe.com

ISBN: 978-0-9944814-0-5 (pbk)
978-0-9944814-1-2 (e-bk)

Dedicated to my children Dearne, Christopher, Rebecca and Marnie-lea.

When silence abounds in its' noisy way,
When creak and cackle and caw of birds
can be heard in a resounding play,
Then chances are good the pathway is clear
for Fear can be felt, smelt and heard,
Sending all, helter skelter,
to find means for shelter,
To hide away, not knowing why,
Until the Fear has passed
and the shadow it had cast.

('Mankind' by D.O'Brien)

(Men know themselves by what they intend, not by what they do)
"And the road to Hell is paved with good intentions"

PROLOGUE

The stones crunched under her feet, skirts swirling around her ankles as she strode down the pitted and cracked driveway, her eyes scanning the dilapidated buildings as she passed by them. She reached the end of the driveway and turned to look around, taking in the rows of old and crumbling buildings. No one seemed to be about, nothing stirred, only the wind rustling the row of big old trees which ran the centre of the driveway to the back buildings, effectively separating the two lines of unit blocks that faced each other. Maybe the place is deserted, maybe nothing lived here, only the impossible number of stray cats she could see looking out at her from under branches and leaves. Looking around, she thought, "Surely, no one could live here." She slowly turned around, taking in the quietness, listening to the rustling foliage, aware of a time past and the splendour that must have once been.

The five acres set in the centre of what is now, a ritzy seaside Holiday Resort Town, with Millionaires and High Flyers in abundance. In the days this Complex was built, it was the only one of its' kind, and was the first to offer such casual seaside opulence.

Now standing in decay, the once perfect pool empty, with dead and dying leaves blowing about the mildewed bottom. The deck chairs, now big clumsy, splintered, wooden things lying about the overgrown lawns. She stood still, listening, then turned and strode back down the driveway from where she had just come, suddenly not wanting to meet anyone anymore, thinking, "No, no one must live here." After all, it was only curiosity that had brought her into the Complex in the first place, the broken and falling down sign out the front reading 'KOINS MOTEL'.

THE OFFICE

The old couple appeared to be arguing, watching them through the glass of the big heavy doors, the wonky hand written sign saying "Office" taped just above the handle, occasionally blocking her view. The door slid open and their conversation tapered off, the old woman becoming aware of one of her tenants waiting patiently to see her. The tenant went over to talk quietly to her, leaving his companion to wait, watching, as he had his quick conversation with her. The old man leaning out of the door to listen to what they said.

She glanced around, feeling a little uncomfortable with her surroundings. The decay was everywhere, and she had seen this place before, not the people though, only the place. She smiled, it is funny how things happen, how things turn out, how you find yourself in the strangest of places, and how you end up somewhere you would never have dreamt of ever going.

The strawberry season was coming to an end, the heat of the Queensland sun building with the change of Seasons. The Pickers knew it would be a matter of only a few weeks of harvesting left before it was too hot for the fruit, and it would be all over again, for another year.

They had been sitting in the shade of a tractor, leaning back on the big mud encrusted wheels, eating lunch and mucking around with each other, relieving the monotony of picking strawberries and stretching sore bent backs. She had spoken of looking for a flat or unit that evening, after work was over for another very long day, and her workmate had said, "Come with me this evening, we have a couple of places available where I live. I'll take you to meet the Landlords."

Now, as she looked around, she was not sure anymore.

Rentals had become increasingly expensive and hard to get in this seaside Resort Town on the Queensland coastline of Australia. Landlords were asking ridiculous prices for their rental properties, and this place did not appear to be any different.

In another time and place, it would have been shameful to put someone in such a place and charge them at all for it, but people were taking advantage of the opportunities, and since everyone was doing it, it seemed less shameful to them. There were still a few who found they had to stand by their integrity, but they were far and few between. Why else be in the Business if not for profit, was the most commonly bartered excuse. It is no place for soft heartedness, after all.

The old woman glanced at her. She could see by the hawk-like intensity of her gaze in that casual glance, this woman never missed anything. A lifetime spent in the scrutiny and the summing up of those around her. Her perceptions now as automatic to her as walking or talking is to others, she trusted them unreservedly, and many had fallen by the wayside, inadvertent victims of nothing more than those trusted and often accurate, assessments.

Getting a 'pass' did not depend on how you looked or what your trade might be, you would be judged on something deeper than that, something only the old woman could see, and if you triggered her Christian responses, the gates would be opened and she would tolerate you in her world. And only then, as long as the limitations imposed on you were well respected.

She appeared to be in her seventies but was in fact, in her eighties, as was her husband of sixty or so years. They were Christians of the old kind. The kind that thought that to believe in Jesus was enough to save you. It did not matter how you behaved in your daily life, or what your intentions or deeds had been about, all of this was irrelevant and made no difference. You only had to believe.

To spend a day on your knees praying for what you want out of life was perfectly acceptable, and in every way was still the cornerstone of their entire lives. As such, every conversation they had, strangers or friends alike, inevitably ended up including a sermon of some kind, for the lost and wayward soul standing before them. It was their duty even, to collect these wayward souls for Jesus, and everyone they met was considered wanting in some way or another.

Their methods, honed by the many years of practised pouncing on the unwary, now a fine art. Skilfully delivered with unexpected ease, often leaving the recipient open mouthed, to consider the truth of how useless they are as people and how unhappy their lives really are, their contentedness evidently, only an illusion.

They had long since gone their own way in the manner in which they practised their religion, and they had built a small Chapel within the grounds of the unit complex. They had made it well known to all of the tenants, that on Sundays there was a Service in the Chapel with a free lunch to follow the Service, and they would take notice of those who chose not to attend, that their attitude towards them would be affected if they indeed, did not attend, as many if not most, did not, preferring to take their chances anyway, the ordeal too much for the life-hardened population at Koins Motel to cope with quietly.

It had been suggested though, by a few of the old Real Estate professionals who had been around since the beginnings of the development and expansion of this beautiful seaside Town, that the Chapel was really the result of a problem with Local Government and the manner in which their Taxing Systems worked, and of how the land became exempt of Land Taxes if it was used for a religious purpose.

These professionals knew the old man and woman well. The old man had a Real Estate License himself, and he too, had worked in the Industry in those days, with the help of his only daughter who had run the Real Estate office which was lodged within the complex, for him. That, over time, they had bought up a good deal of local Real Estate and now, in their eighties, were considered by most to own half of the Town, with their worth running into the multi-millions.

The old man did not consider any of this to be contradictory to their religious beliefs, or that the very nature of flogging property to the uninformed or vulnerable, meant anything much at all. If anyone was hurt in these processes, it was only because they did not believe, and therefore, were not saved.

The niche they had made for themselves in their chosen way of life, was comfortable indeed.

He had spent many a Friday evening standing in front of the local Pub, loudly preaching reform against the evil grog and to go home to your families, but that was the sixties and seventies, or so. He found other ways to pay his dues nowadays, and Sunday Service, for which he was the Preacher and Sermon bringer, was just one of those ways.

"You're looking for a unit?" the old woman, not looking up, called towards her.

"Yes," she replied, choosing to keep her conversation to a minimum until she had decided to commit to this strange derelict world and these odd archaic people, who could have stepped straight out of a time now long past, the sounds of then still murmuring softly around them.

"We have a couple available after this weekend. Wait there a minute and I will take you down the back. I can show you from the outside what will be available. You work in the strawberry fields? I love strawberries. Are you doing seven days? Must be good money……" the barrage trailed off, still the old woman did not look up.

Lulled by the continuous litany, and bone tired from the long and demanding day, she missed her moment to respond, finally realising it was her turn to speak and only managing a few nods of her head. The old woman took no notice.

A few minutes later, the office door reluctantly grated open on unoiled sliders again, the old woman stepped out. She could see the old man looking her over from the now shadowy interior of the small office. She glanced over her shoulder, realising that twilight was fast becoming the dark of night.

Leaving the old man behind, they walked down the pitted and crumbling driveway, just the two of them, towards the unit blocks at the back of the Complex. Her attention focussed on her feet, trying not to trip over the raised cracks or stumble on rubble, aware of how nimble the eighty odd year old woman was managing with ease to navigate her way in the dark, idly chatting as she walked and always two steps ahead in her confident journey over well familiar ground.

She realised the old woman was giving her a bit of a run-down on the general layout of the complex, "These are two bedrooms, this one is a self-contained cottage but they have been there a long time," and on and on it went. She smiled, if the old woman began the telling of the occupants' life stories too, she did not know what she would do. She tried harder to focus her tired mind, the pitted path and her unsure footing distracting her further.

They reached the end of the driveway and the old woman pointed to a door with a wobbly '14' hand painted on it in large white, chipped numerals.

"This one is a standard Motel room, it is the cheapest type we have," she stated firmly.

"It's available this weekend. The fellow is behind in his rent, he has until this weekend to move out or we will change the locks and I will confiscate his belongings!" she had cautiously lowered her voice, her eyes not leaving the closed door as if expecting him to burst through it at any moment.

"He has been nothing but trouble, never there when you try to speak with him, but he knows he has to go," she stated as a matter of fact, all just business.

They walked on, coming to stand outside another door. There was a similar large wobbly white '16' painted on the door.

"This one is a single bedroom unit with its' own kitchen. It is dearer than the other one, but it's empty now. One of our tenants' is cleaning it for me and he will be finished in the next few days. By this weekend, anyhow," she said. "Which one do you want?" she asked, her tone suggesting there was no question that she would indeed, choose one or the other.

"I'll take the smaller one, thanks," she replied, at once considering how much she was prepared to pay for such accommodation and deciding the higher amount was pushing it too far. Not because she did not have it, but because she just found it too objectionable to pay so high a price for what she was looking at. Not sure how anyone could put such prices on them and not be embarrassed to do so. She was to learn, embarrassment was hard to find around here.

As if an after-thought she said, "There is supposed to be no cooking in the Motel rooms. We approached the Council but they would not give permission for cooking in any of the rooms without kitchens," the old woman lent towards her, conspiratorially she whispered, "We tell everyone to just do it anyway, and that we know nothing about it. We have given nobody permission to cook in their unit. Understand?" Her raised eyebrow supporting the emphasis placed on the 'understand?'

"I understand!" "Thank You," she added, realising suddenly that her lack of commitment or involvement, was going to have to be a way of life here, for a while anyway.

And, she did understand. She understood that encouraging others to fib had nothing to do with Christian ethics if it suited a personal cause, or so it seemed. When walking on glass, walk carefully.

"Well, come back up to the office and we will sort the paperwork out. You have Bond? It will be two weeks in advance and four weeks Bond. You won't have trouble with that, will you? The Bond is yours of course, it is only held for you and you get it back …." The old woman, needing to take a breath, trailed off again. Already two steps ahead again as she sped on, back toward the little office at the head of the main driveway.

The old man was waiting for them at the great glass doors. "How'd it go, you taking it?" he called to them as they approached. "Which one?" he added, as confidant she would choose one or the other.

"Yes, thank you. The little one," she replied, settling into the polite responses that would be her habit from now on.

"You'll be right, come on in and tell me all about yourself, you work in the strawberry fields, hey?" "With Mickie!" he finished, his tone confirming an approval for the recommendation having come from a known tenant.

The quiet, studious manner of before was now gone, she noticed.

"You must come to Church on Sundays. We have lunch as well, everyone is welcome. We invite any of the homeless in the area to come if they want to," he said, almost proudly.

The homeless rarely did come she would discover, and she would soon find out why that was.

"You believe in Jesus?" he continued almost conversationally, taking her by surprise.

"You won't be saved if you don't believe in Jesus," he stated factually, his eyebrows rising slightly as he looked down at her with heavy lidded eyes, still sharp and clear for one carrying such age.

She watched the old lady fishing in drawers, getting papers together and appearing to generally fiddle about. Wishing she would hurry up, eager to get this done and be on her way, especially if this was to spiral into anything even remotely resembling a class on Religious principles.

She was wilting after the hot, back breaking day in the fields. Beginning her day with a 5 a.m. start and not finishing until 6 p.m., then the little bus that took them to, and collected them from the fields, taking its' hour long bumpy, swaying ride back to Town. It was a punishing, long daily process. The last thing she wanted was a discussion on Jesus, or the competitiveness that seemed always to be a part of such deals. Although, she was aware that this man was not looking for a discussion, he was telling her, and his attitude suggested he would brook no arguments about it.

So, she smiled, she nodded, offering very little that might encourage him on, only saying how spiritual she was, that she had spent her Primary School years in a Catholic Convent, taught by Nuns and "Yes," she knew her Bible (well, somewhat, it had been a long time since then).

Her revelations only opening another unexpected can of worms, as he told her, "Yes, but do you believe in Jesus? You don't need all that other sort of hoopla. You only have to believe in Jesus!" "That's all you need!" he said with renewed vigour.

Grateful for the reprieve as the old woman placed the paperwork on the table in front of her. Finally, the papers were signed, the money was paid. She could go get some much needed R and R.

The old couple called out their "Goodbye" and "See you on Saturday!"

The old man looking particularly chuffed to have another room taken care of, and before the old tenant had even moved out. His pleasure showing in the way he had affectionately placed a hand on her departing back.

Keen to get away before anything else might hold her up, she lifted her hand in a wave as she called back to them, "See you Saturday, Mr and Mrs Koin."

BUFF

Standing in the middle of the little room that was once an opulent Motel room, her bag discarded on the double bed which took up most of the space, she idly assessed her surroundings. Not in any hurry, able to take her own time, she familiarised herself with her new home.

The little microwave oven that had seen better days, the old television, and a small bedside table covered in scratches and graffiti were the only other things in the tiny and compact room.

The light sea breeze coming in the large open sliding windows was gently lifting the tattered and dust covered curtains. The musky smell of the ancient worn carpets, made worse with the heat of the day, was overpowering to her. The yellowing peeling paint hanging in ripped brittle shards here and there, off the pock marked and grime covered walls.

She could see daylight around the closed, ill-fitting, flimsy front door that had been hanging there since biblical days and looked like a good lean on it would force it open. A hefty kick would pop it off its' rusty hinges, altogether. An indented hole in the middle of it, confirmed a moment of violence from a well-placed foot at some time or other, in its' long history.

The bathroom was at the far end of the room, noticing that at least it looked clean enough, although she would scrub it with bleach before she was prepared to use it. She counted the missing tiles off the walls for no other reason than a distracted effort to take stock of her surroundings. Wandering around, looking at broken catches on windows and cracked panes and putting off any thoughts of where to begin the inevitable scrubbing she would have to do over the next few days.

The mattress was another story again. She would not use the disgustingly filthy thing, covered in all sorts of grunge, and she was sure, a massive patch of old dried blood taking up most of it's centre. She could only imagine the kind of bugs that must infest it now, and the only place it was fit for was the rubbish skip out on the roadway. To think she should ask permission to throw it away maddened her. "Like bloody hell she would," she had thought to herself.

This was to be her home, for what would turn out to be, the next eighteen months, and so far removed from what she was accustomed to, that in her innocence, she could view this as a great adventure, make the best of it, see where life leads, and all that sort of stuff. Free of the commitments and responsibility for others for the first time in her adult life, feeding her enthusiasm for the unknown.

It was a peculiar feeling, being able to make her own choices, and to come and go as she wanted. Not having to check in with anyone, or fit in with their wants and needs, or to pay those Bills for everyone else. To answer the door, pick up the phone, all of those little things in her life until now, dictated by others and their schedules and commitments. Even as a child nothing was ever up to her. Being an only child, and as such, wrapped in cotton wool by over-protective parents, she was always chaperoned, no matter where she went.

So, it was mildly soothing and not really frightening at all. A clean slate. A new beginning, where all the old rules had changed. The boundaries were set by her now, not by others. The money she earned, for the first time ever, was all hers to do with or not, as she wanted. The dinner she ate, the time she ate it, eating it at all, all up to her for the first time, also. Almost as if the Clock of Ages had taken a turn, dragging everything with it, unresisting, into the next Age.

It was hard to believe such simple things could mean so much, or bring liberty and the feeling of freedom to anyone, but they did.

It was easy to imagine this great adventure, since she had nothing else with which to gauge it on, and to press on with no thought at all, to the dangers that may be ahead.

Hearing voices outside, her evaluations and brief reverie disturbed, she looked out of one of the large windows. There, standing together in casual conversation, were two men. One very tall blonde man of around forty, dressed in what looked like a Boy Scout uniform, and the other by contrast, was a very short, very thin, scrawny man in his sixties.

The short man, she surmised, must be Buff.

The Koins had told her he was living in the room next to her. He was their Maintenance Man come Caretaker and general Dogsbody, for which he received a lowered rent in return for his services but no actual money, and he would keep an eye out for her, that she should make herself known to him, first chance. For some reason that she was not sure of, the 'should' sounded more like an instruction at the time, enough so anyway, that it had caught her attention.

In time, she came to realise that he would already have known all about her. The hovering outside her room was his way of letting her have the opportunity to come out and introduce herself, that there was nothing that went on in this place which was unknown to him, or ever got past him.

He was their, not so covert, informant, keeping them on top of all the comings and goings. Little did they suspect he always chose carefully what they were told and how they were told it, and that he used this privilege to gain authority over the other tenants. It paid to stay on his good side, and everyone knew it. For any new ones, he made sure they knew it soon enough.

She did not know who the other man was, and she had not considered for a moment that he might be a tenant. He looked too affluent and tidy in his neatly pressed uniform, to be someone who would want to live amidst the broken and decaying ruins of this place.

She watched as the blonde man in his crisp uniform walked away. Thinking, "Oh well, here goes," opening her door, she went outside.

"Hello, you must be Buff. The Koins told me I must come and meet you," she called to him.

He glanced back over his shoulder to look at her. He had been standing, hands on hips, watching the blonde man making his way towards the main roadway, a small smile playing on his curled lips.

He grinned at her.

"Yes. Am pleased to meet you. Saw you come in. The Koins tell me you're in the strawberry fields, come sit and talk to me." It seemed this habit of rushing to say everything at once, was catching. He sounded just like Mr and Mrs Koin. Sounded like some pruned and puckered, over-aged child wanting to mimic its' parents. She stifled her wide grin at the image this induced, hiding it behind a warmer than was needed, greeting. Her enthusiasm purposefully distracting him.

They moved to the ancient, overworked and somewhat wonky outdoor table with slab seats attached, which was placed perfectly, right in front of her room. Similarly, with most of the other rooms, she saw as she looked around.

They sat together, talking in general. She let him take the lead and politely followed his line of preferred conversation.

He told her a little about the place, and how she was to be cautious at all times, of the 'type of people' who were tenants there. She was not to trust anyone, not anyone, ever! He said this with a firm voice and a stern look, wanting his warning to be clear, expecting her to take him seriously, in this well-meaning bit of advice.

She wondered if that caution should include him too.

He also told her that if she was to need anything fixed or work done, she was not to bother the Koins, she was to come to him, and he would look after it for her. He would always see her right. There was never any need to bother the Koins when she could come to him, that's what he was there for after all, and he was always happy to oblige anyone in distress, he said.

His heavily lined face showing the years of boozing. His skin the colour of yellow mustard, told her he was not a healthy man. She sensed he was protective of his position, and his attitude, the cocky, confident way he held his roll-your-own cigarette, spoke loudly of the satisfaction he gleaned from his authority over others there, and the recognition they accorded him for his status. He would never relinquish it easily.

She also recognised that this was a common symptom of very short, small men, and she had seen it often enough before. But now running rampant, in a perfect marriage with the position he held in the Complex feeding it freely, and going unchecked by any outside circumstances.

He told her how he had once been a Mechanic in his young working life. How, he still fixed cars for friends on the side and that was why the area in front of his room had no outside table, having to keep the area clear for any cars that may come in, and that he would share her table with her. Like it or not she realised, and as she was to find out, it was a sharing that could be a real nuisance, when his mates would show up for a louder than life, early morning get together, right in front of her door.

He showed her a long scar running the full length of the back of one of his legs. He'd had an unexpected, near fatal attack, causing an urgent Bypass heart operation, and that was what had finally retired him, fated now to a life on a Disability Pension.

"I didn't ask for that to happen to me, did I, hey? Did I!?" he said to her, his voice rising with a whining pitch. "Wasn't my choice, the Doctor said no more work. Not my choice at all!" he almost spat out, as if getting rid of something distasteful in his mouth, his nose screwed up.

She wondered if a life of heavy drinking and heavy smoking was also 'not his choice,' but she knew better than to say it.

He told her of his only child, a daughter, who lived nearby with her husband, no children.

How, his ex-wife, when she had passed on, had left their house to the daughter, who promptly sold it to build the house they now live in. How, he had given it to his ex-wife in a Divorce Settlement and how it had originally belonged to his parents, but, "Well, that's the way it goes. I'm not complaining," he had said rather too forcefully to sound true.

He told her how his very religious daughter was too unwell to have him living with them. How, they had tried it once for a while, and how it had ultimately become too much for her to cope with, even though he'd had his own little granny flat downstairs, and how he had finally had to move out. How, in her well moments, they often went to Timor with their Church to help the natives there, and that one day, he would go to Timor, too.

She felt a little sorry for him, and she wondered at the degrees of conscience some people had.

They sat for quite a while, more him chatting and her listening, sipping some sort of thick coffee. An occasional person or two strolled past now and then, calling out their greetings to Buff as they went by, no one game to offend this little man who had the ear of the Koins and thus, the control of their comfortable future and the roof over their heads in his hands. Nobody stopped to talk, although all of them gave her a good look-over, curious, but not enough to disturb Buff's time with her.

She would be the talk of the whole place soon, and she knew they would all come, bit by bit, to check out the new person who had come into their world. Only a close-up perusal would gift her an okay to carry on, from those living in this confined and dangerous environment.

She decided she would not look a gift horse in the mouth, in being given a room next to Buff. She would befriend, to a degree, this sad, lonely little man, who seemed quietly unable to believe the hand that life had dealt him, or to figure out how it had come about, that he had so little now when he had once had so much, and she made a point of having a coffee with him whenever she could, giving him her ear at those times. But she never forgot the wise warning of caution, for she had also seen the pleasure he garnered from the power and influence he wielded, over those whose lives he had so much control over. She knew that while he could feel sorry for his own lot in life, he was not prepared to give the same considerations to those around him now. His enjoyment of the prestige was far more worthwhile to him, than the digging he would have to do, to find pity for anyone else. Spite, was his form of revenge on the unfair world he alone, lived in.

There would be no empathy for any, from this little man.

Having had enough, she chose her moment to make a move. Telling him it was time to get on with things that needed doing, and that she was close by if he should need to find her for anything. Helpfulness, the bridge she would stand on, to ward away any real curiosity.

The day was a beautiful balmy day, with a breeze that smelt of salt. The type of day that was most common this part of the Queensland coastline and easy to become immune to, only noticing the days that were not so balmy and beautiful, mainly during the Cyclone season up north, with the effects of such tropical weather occasionally felt this far south.

But that was only now and then, over a few months or so of the year, and was something you accepted if you were a long-time Queenslander. 'Beautiful one day – Perfect the next' the tourist slogan went, or something like that.

Spoilt? You bet!

She had been keeping to herself mostly, since moving in. Taking the time to get to know her surroundings and watching carefully, the comings and goings around her.

It was obvious to her, that the diversity of people who lived at the Complex was as great and far ranging in ages and lifestyle types, as you could get anywhere, but they all seemed to have one thing in common – they were forced to live in such a place because of the way the high rents for little in return, now restricted their ability to pick and choose the quality of their living conditions. The frustrations and lack of patience this produced in everyone, was a palpable thing, and made for some very pissed off and nasty tempered people, everywhere. The feelings of dislike, and opposition for the huge loss of money for that little in return, with the animosity growing daily, was turned outward and expressed vocally and frequently. And over the most benign of things, most times.

Only those who had bought Real Estate back in the days when it was a sleepy little, harder to get to, fishing village, with only a handful of locals who actually lived there then and were not just passing through on their way to somewhere else, were laughing loudly nowadays with many of the new Millionaires being made from an original investment of anything between a paltry $25,000 for vacant land and $45-60,000 for a standing home.

She remembered how cheap you could pick a place up for just twenty years or so ago, but like a lot of others, had declined the opportunity because you 'wouldn't want to live there,' 'it's too far away from the big City', 'the bloody sand flies are shockers with of all that scrub around,' 'you could only use it for holidays and who would rent it long term,' and so on and on. Those, without the vision to see how time would grow such areas no matter what, had missed out big time, for sure.

Well, that was the nature of progress. Happened that way all over the world. No exceptions here. Why should there be?

It was those cheap prices, and the building of a major Highway leading north from Brisbane by-passing all the coastal Towns along the way, that had gained the interest of the big Developers. The potential was now worth the risk.

That was okay. As it should be really, but all of that not changing the position which everyone, both working and living here, now faced.

Long term residents who had called this part of the world their home for many years, now could not afford to live here, along with the migrating fruit Pickers and Workers whose services were greatly relied upon by the many fruit and vegetable Farms which lay inland and behind the seaside and coastal Towns. All, were now in the same boat.

The perfect storm - the greedy and unethical come out of the woodwork everywhere, pushing the prices even higher and dropping acceptable standards at the same time. And, the less fortunate, hard done-by's and hard workers, get rorted. Those, who can no longer match the high prices, go homeless.

Not wanting to waste a rare day off, she wandered down to the shore and sat, looking out to sea. With the multitude of hi-rise apartments and concrete towers at her back, a big freighter heading north went past on its' lumbering journey to the only docks that could accommodate it's huge size, a little further up the picturesque coastline.

It is funny how you get so used to something, you end up taking it for granted. She could not remember at all, the last time she actually went swimming or had gotten into the ocean and braved its' foaming waves.

The wind surfers were everywhere. Little flying figures, hanging so helplessly under great canopies. People, on enthusiastically looked forward to holidays, laughing and frolicking about happily, with joyfully playing children digging in the white sand, were a contrast to the dirty, scruffy homeless man on his way to nowhere.

She watched his shuffling, staggered steps, until he turned a bend and was gone.

CHURCH

The strawberry season was over with Spring catching hold of the days. Now, the heat was becoming more intense as the weeks turned over, drawing Christmas closer and closer, bringing the Cyclone season up north with it, and the very height of Summer.

She had lost her excuse of work finally, for not attending a Sunday Service now and then, but she had been curious enough to see what it was all about and so she did not really mind going along, just once or twice, anyway. Confident, she could control the persuasive influences of the Koins, she lined up for her first visit, believing she would be excused whenever it suited her.

The tiny Chapel beside the Koins' cottage, with the sad, peeling paint on the sign tucked up under the eaves reading 'Deliverance Hall', was jammed full of old furniture and used mattresses spread around and pushed up against the walls. Only a little walking space was left in the middle for the two rows of decrepit, unmatched chairs facing each other. The dilapidated upright piano in one corner still worked well enough to provide a bit of a tune when it was needed, or when Mr and Mrs Koins daughter was visiting, her, usually being the only one about who could still make it produce something akin to music.

The first thing to hit her senses, other than the chaotic mass of furniture, was the ancient smell of the place, made fierce by the rising heat of the Summer days. The building always locked up tight on every other day and opened only on Sundays, did not help, either. A table at one end held tea cups and saucers, a hot water urn, cakes and packets of cheap bulk meat pies, all waiting for the Sermons to be over, when everyone could have something to eat. A reward for attending, and the only real reason an occasional few homeless people ever came along.

Everyone was handed one of the numerous and varied old Bibles on their way in, so they could follow for themselves whatever verse Mr Koin had chosen to read to them that day. The one thing the Bibles all did have in common, was the size of the tiny print, which made it all the more amazing that the eighty odd year old Mr Koin, would read from these pages without the use of eye glasses, causing her to wonder if he was really reading from memory, with all those long years of well-performed daily use behind him.

Once, when she declined to take a turn reading the chosen verses, saying she did not have her glasses with her, she was handed a rather large, rather ancient magnifying glass with an oversized handle. After stuttering her way through all of it, she was never asked to do so again on any of her subsequent visits. Sometimes, there is something to be said for inadequacies. She had smiled, with only a small pang of guilt for the manipulation.

On the few times she attended these Meetings, while there were a few regulars who went every Sunday, those, who enjoyed the free lunch and who seemed to semi sleep through the rest of the affair, the other participants were always new to her.

A local homeless girl, who everyone knew by sight, came once. She had a serious problem with the drink. With all her money going on booze, she was often seen being tossed out of a local Business, generally a Bakery or something similar, where she had thrown a tantrum, chucking chairs and tables around because they had refused to give her a pie, or something else to eat. Occasionally, the Police would be there, after the Owner had decided he had been generous enough, over the all too many other times he had fed her, and fearing for the safety of his other patrons, had given up wanting to, or trying to, control her violent and verbal eruptions.

It did not help her cause either, when everyone knew the money she received from the Government, not to mention the money she earned prostituting, all went on booze. Sometimes other types of drugs too, but only because of the company she might be with at the time, and her need to be one of their accepted crowd. Occasionally, on days in between their payments of Government money, the gathering of a little group could be seen on a street corner or in the middle of a park, pooling whatever money they had, to buy whatever they could, and their purchases would be shared out fairly amongst all of them. A staunch group, self-supporting and united in their mutual needs. It was at these times that she would be involved in the purchase of drugs rather than booze, wanting to do her bit for the only family she had.

She was of medium height, but her skeletal form made her appear taller than she was. Great black rings around her sunken eyes stood out against the pallid skin hanging on her bones. Her short ashy blonde hair stood up in dirty, oily spikes around her head. For a girl of only thirty or so, she looked much older and nearer to death than she should for one still so young. The look of hopelessness always on her gaunt face, with a sadness that swirled around her and a stale smell that followed in her wake. There was never a time when anyone had seen her sober, and no one knew her real personality, or what her past was all about. There were rumours she had a family somewhere, who had tried many times to help her, but who knew the truth of these rumours.

It was no surprise then, when Mr Koin seemed to forget the usual verse reading that Sunday, choosing instead, to hone in on the girl as soon as she sat down, having appeared in the doorway just after the Service had begun. Hesitating, unsure of her walk amongst these strangers.

After encouraging her to come in and sit herself down, without giving her more than a moment to settle, he had begun by asking her how many cigarettes she would smoke in a day. When she answered that she did not know, he asked her why she did not know. The girl, looking around forlornly at the other attendants as if beseeching them for their aid, answering that it depended on how much she'd had to drink and that for the most part, she could never remember when she'd had the last cigarette.

'Oops!' everyone had thought at the time, throwing covert glances at each other.

Encouraged by her answer, this line of questioning went on for some ten or fifteen minutes, interspersed with quotes from the Bible and a few 'don't you know that..,' along with it.

Everyone else sat silently, feeling uncomfortable and helpless, listening to the interrogation, knowing better than to even try to interfere.

Finally, the girl, unable to hide her embarrassment and shame, saying nothing else, jumped up and raced outside, never to be seen there again. She had lasted all of twenty minutes or so, and had not had the something to eat which she had come for, in the first place.

After Mr Koin had pointed out to the silent audience that she was a hopeless lost cause, he went on with his Reading as if nothing had ever disturbed it.

On another Sunday, the Service was forgotten altogether when the Police had to be called to come rescue everyone who was attending.

Another young homeless fellow, who had been prowling around the Complex for a few weeks, sometimes sleeping up under the outdoor awning in the pool area, sometimes someone who was curious enough to speak with him, offering up their couch for the night, came to have something to eat and went through a similar process as the girl had previously. This fellows' problem was a drug addiction and not just booze. Ice, was his favoured choice, and as such, he was as temperamental and short-fused as you could get, with an acute jealous streak for anyone who lived a normal and uncontaminated life. Often suffering moments of ferocious temper, he was one to be avoided, and certainly never provoked.

Instead of him storming off in his annoyance, he decided to attack the Koins' Mercedes, which was parked in the driveway beside the Chapel rather than its' usual safe place in the garage. Repeatedly kicking it, and when he tired of that, whacking it with a large stone, cursing and screaming unintelligible things with each smack, his temper rising with every blow.

When he turned his attention to the Koins themselves, the doors were quickly locked against him. This only infuriated and frustrated him more, so he went on to try to kick the great wooden doors in, and no one being prepared to open the only safety barrier between them and him, and go outside to try and pacify the out of control maniac, Mr Koin promptly called the Police, who, after subduing him in their determined and forceful way, took him away and charged him for all his vicious efforts.

A few days later, regardless of the Restraining Order he had been given by the Court, the young fellow showed up at the Office door to ask, not too politely, why they had called the Police and had him charged, to which the Police promptly came again and took him away. This time, he did not come back and another of the random campers about the place was finally gone, much to the relief of many of the tenants who, frightened by his manic behaviour, had begun to avoid him when they saw him coming their way.

On another occasion, one of those random campers, one who managed to withstand the usual interrogation, was a young needle addict who was heavily pregnant. She sat tiredly and silently through it all, and she was happy to have something to eat when all of the Sermons had finally petered out. Eating her meal quietly, not knowing when her next meal might come, intent on every mouthful, she sat in a corner on her own. Gladly, she followed her cheap packet pie and vegetables with a big piece of cake and a hot cup of tea. Savouring the prize for her endurance and patience, and living proof that one could prevail, if you just held on long enough. That, eventually, Mr Koin had to pack it in, the clock ticking over, after all.

She was camping out, under a big tree, in a small piece of tarp thrown over a branch, behind the end units that backed onto the rear boundary. Trying to be as invisible as she could, quietly wanting to hide the fact she was there, but while everyone knew it anyway, nobody offered her their assistance or shelter. Because, the girl was on her third pregnancy and that by her choice, the baby would be taken into Foster Care when it was born, along with the two other older siblings who had come into the world in the same fashion. Because, she refused any aid from the Care facilities that the Government offered to one such as herself, preferring not to give up her addiction and wanting to stay on the streets. Because, she spent all of her Government money on her drugs, which was a substantial enough amount to have provided her enough money for housing and food, she had lost the sympathy and support of all of the tenants.

Most of them, knowing of her and her previous history, their disgust barely hidden and finding it difficult if not impossible, not to side with the little unborn baby over her lack of concern for its' welfare and well-being. Selfish bitch, a few of the older men would say loudly whenever they saw her, their glares warning her of her unwelcome standing amongst them.

On this Sunday, Mr Koin remarking, when she had left after having her something to eat, that "they should tie that girls tubes instead of allowing these continual pregnancies."

She had smiled at the comment, not sure who the 'They' was.

She felt sorry for the girl, and she asked her whenever she saw her if she was alright, and was there anything she could do for her. The offer was always declined with a wave of the hand, and finally with some frustration, the girl whispering to her that she would do her a better service, if she was to just pretend she was not there at all. All the time looking down at her dirty feet working circles into the dry, dusty dirt, she waited quietly for a nod or a commitment of some kind, an agreement to leave her be.

Not long after this, she disappeared back onto the streets after her baby was born, and she never saw her again.

This one hurt the heart a little. Not only for such a young woman who would live this short and sad life, but for another little baby coming into the world with the hard fight of an addict before them.

It did not take any effort at all to decide it was all too much for her, these 'Sunday Services.' Finding them emotionally gruelling rather than the calm Spiritual comfort one should expect a Sunday Service to be. A quiet interlude and a place of support, away from the rigors of daily life, where any judgements are left to God, and she began to make excuses for her absences, after this.

ALEXANDER

The tap, tap, tap of the metal end of the splintered old walking stick heralded the impending arrival at her door, of Alexander. A man of middle age, he used his walking stick when getting about the Complex, but if he went out onto the streets, he used his creaking antique motorised chair. Looking like some crazed extra straight out of Mad Max, with its' big wheels covered in strange graffiti written on bits of paper or material, and woven between the spikes. A little flag pole with a football pendant flapping from the top rose up behind his head where it competed for space with the splintered, chipped walking stick with the lethal metal tip. Never too far from his hand, the stick was a perfect weapon for self-protection as well, should one ever be needed out on the streets he would argue, if anyone was ever interested enough to listen.

Although, she thought the image of Alexander chasing anyone, hopping on his gummy leg, arm raised, brandishing his metal tipped walking stick was so funny that anyone would laugh themselves to death, more so, than there being any chance of finding any other fatal end at the hands of a rampaging Alexander.

There was not a lot wrong with Alexander. Only a slight limp from a bad leg, but he had achieved a Disability Pension anyway, allowing him to indulge himself in his red wine and the precious pills that dictated the terms of his whole life.

Everyone knew, that for the most part, his routine was to sleep all day and stay up all night (that wonderful aloneness, the 'nobody can see me,' quiet of the night) when he would drink his wine and constantly pop his pills until he was satisfied that he had reached the stage he wanted to be at, and then some more, just for good measure. Yet, she knew, he often peeked through his closed curtains during the day, and he saw a good deal more of what was going on than he would ever admit to, to anyone else. He enjoyed, and nurtured, his invented role of helplessness and innocence, as delusional as it might be. A delusion that fooled nobody in its obviousness.

He had been a resident at the Complex for a lot of years, and he was a wealth of knowledge on the history of the place, but he had an all abiding dislike for the Koins, mainly stemming from his open and noisily proclaimed covetousness of their wealth, and, not to forget, the pristine Mercedes they often passed by in. He never missed an opportunity, no matter how small, to get at them.

In a way, she understood his animosity. His room was one of the bigger units, with its' own kitchen and laundry, for which he paid a premium rate, but it was also one of the most derelict. With so much needing repair, added to by his own unclean habits and lack of interest, he lived in utter filth.

"You there, girl?" he yelled as he reached her open door.

"I've bought you the local paper, it was in the mailbox, got some good Specials this week!" he followed, with this usual and expected excuse, to find himself at her door.

The food Specials from the local Supermarket changed from week to week, and Alexander was 'on it,' although she did not know why.

He rarely had more than a sandwich to eat, and only now and then, at that. More, the booze specials that were advertised in the same paper she suspected, and the valid excuse it would give him, to come over for a bit of a gossip and a 'did you know?!'

"Did you see the two young couples who moved into these two units next to you?" he asked her when he reached her door, not pausing.

She never asked anyone inside her room, rather, going outside to sit at the outdoor table with them if she wanted to spend some time, or just standing at her door, if she did not. By using this technique, she stayed in control of how much she wanted to give of herself to anyone, and it gave them all the distinct impression that she was a loner. She hung with no one, and because she did not pick and choose alliances, they all accepted her independence and left her alone.

Blending into the background was as good a form of protection as you could get. Nobody noticed you. Especially, when amongst those whose curiosity was created and fed, from a need to protect themselves. A motivation always to be respected, if you knew what was good for you.

"Hmmm, I did Alexander and thank you for the paper," she said, offering no other encouragement.

She stayed at her door this time, having other things to do, but moreover, not wanting to look like she always took up the chance for a chat about others. Something that was always noticed, she had found, and it would add to ones' reputation amongst the other tenants, and never for the good. Everyone knew Alexander was a bit of an old woman and loved a gossip, but everyone forgave him this. They would not be so generous with her, she knew.

"They're young, hey? They are two separate couples, even though they moved in at the same time, they don't know each other, did you know that?" he asked her, seeking more to gauge the level of her knowledge rather than just for conversation.

Not waiting for her answer, he went quickly on, "I tell you what though, that blonde bird knows how to swear, don't she? Fuck this, fuck that, every second word is a Fuck! Do you have to listen to that all the time? How you going to handle that, drive you mad, it would!?" Finally, he stopped for a breath, his mischievous grin slowly appearing, unable to control his mirth at her possible discomfort.

She knew he was fishing. She knew it was Alexanders' way of stirring the pot also. "Yep, I've heard her. Shame, how so many of the younger people fall into that habit, nowadays," she replied without any real commitment.

In truth, heard her, was an understatement. The walls between the rooms may as well have been paper, and it was all she could hear. All anyone could hear, she believed. The young woman, speaking as if she was calling down the length of a football field all the time, did not help the cause either.

Alexander smiled at her. She could see that sly, sideways look he often had when he was being his playful and up to trouble, self. Openly displayed this time, he could not help himself, his planned discretion, if he ever had any, quickly going out the door when he did not get the rise he wanted.

Here we go, she thought. Alexander has found something he thinks he can get his teeth into, for some reason. The woman's ability for swearing, she would bet on. It did not warrant a mention about the blokes around the place who were equally as bad, but that was typical, she knew. This outwardly modern Society not so modern, when push came to shove.

She had given up trying to figure out what drove some of the shit stirrers around the Complex. Boredom probably, more than anything else. A life defined by very small walls.

Today, she was in a hurry, so she was not going to pick any of it up, feigning ignorance to his behaviour. Something she would generally always do in a place such as this, and she was well practised. It was also true she reaped a little satisfaction from his frustration over her not biting, too. Never, ever, get involved.

"I have to go, Alexander! We can catch up some other time, OK? Sorry darlin, but I'm on a timetable today!" she said firmly, a tone that meant 'don't argue,' and was her last and final line of defence against the determined.

She watched him limp his way back across to his own unit. His frame hunched over, the great hump between his shoulder blades aiding the illusion of him wrapping himself around the handle of his walking stick. His sticky, thin black hair hanging in clumped tangles to his shoulders. The thick, black rimmed glasses riding so low on his nose looked as if they might just slide off at any moment. Subconsciously, he lifted his free hand to shove them back onto his nose. They slid back down again. Picking his speed up when he realised his own next door neighbour had come to sit outside.

Thinking distractedly, as she gathered her things into her bag readying herself to go out, "What does it take to make an 'Alexander' what he is?" He would offer to buy a chosen few, always females, a new mobile phone, and, as they would discover if they took him up on the offer, only in order to send them texts full of profanities about the other tenants. Profanities so bad, it was nothing to see someone over there, standing at his door, telling him to "bugger off!" with the shocking texts he was sending their way continuously. You would know the victim of his latest generosity just by whoever was there, yelling at him, now.

He almost had his head bashed in one night, when his neighbours to one side were having a rip roaring domestic at

12 o'clock at night, and Alexander sent them an extensive and vulgar text telling the husband to "give the bitch heaps!"

Dan was renowned for his aggressive moments, and at the time, was on a Good Behaviour Bond with the Courts. While he was well known to the Cops for his strong arm tactics and standover ways, he was terrified of his plump little Mrs, who had a nasty mouth and a nasty disposition, made worse, by her lack of patience for having to chase a little two year old girl around. The Mrs picked the phone up when the text came through, and after reading it, was beside herself over being called a bitch by an intruding Alexander. She yelled and screamed at Dan about it, their previous barny forgotten, until Dan stormed next door, stood over Alexander, who, luckily for him, was sitting in his wheel chair, and threatened to punch him out. Promising that he would, if he ever sent them any texts, of any kind, again.

Any females on their own soon found Alexander was not the perfect confidant either, and any who were separated or divorced, wished they had never told him their Surnames or where they had previously lived. Only discovering the error of this lapse in their caution, when it was too late.

Alexander would spend time with them on many social occasions, full glasses in hand, getting to know them, and he was probably able to get closer to them than most others might, their motherly instincts coming to the fore with his apparent helplessness. Their guards dropping, unsuspectingly giving him all the fuel he needed to create his little fires.

One, in particular, was to really regret their early association. Rita moved into the unit on the other side of Alexander, after separating with her husband of twenty years. She was in her early forties, with a heavy and sometimes unfathomable, Dutch accent. After years of the restrictions which come with married life, she tended to let her hair down now and then. Letting it down with her new neighbour, who was happy to encourage her, was something she did on many an evening. Until, one day, when she came running over upset and crying, with a letter flapping in her hand from a very irate and disbelieving, ex-husband.

Alexander had looked up the ex-husbands' address from his name on the Electoral Rolls, and he had written a very expressive letter to him. Full of all sorts of colourful language, condemning her frequently drunken behaviour, and complaining of her oft attendance at his door. Of how, he thought he was doing the ex-husband a favour in letting him know of this loose woman's antics, who he was blessed to no longer be married to. How, maybe, his letter to him would aid the ex-husband in his enterprises through the Divorce Courts.

That was the end of what had seemed to be, a developing and genuine friendship of kindred spirits, both, with their own disadvantages in life.

Anyway, this being the nature of Alexander, it was no surprise then, when one day, all those who were home came outside to watch, smirking, while two young Policemen standing at his door, threatened to knock it down, if he did not open it.

Two days before this well-watched event, she had been on her way home after being away for a few days, and as it was closer to her bus stop, she had chosen the main entrance rather than her preferred and more discreet alternative side entrance off the back road.

Passing the Office doors, she saw that the daughters' Mercedes was parked there and that her and her family must be on one of their visits for the weekend. The monthly journey of a few hundred kilometres, made regularly, from their massive Cotton farm in the Hinterland behind the City, but she had not noticed the young man in navy blue overalls, leaning over the bonnet and windscreen of the Mercedes, with a small brush in one hand, until she was right on top of him.

She paused to collect her mail from the box set into the Office wall, giving him an interested once over, a quick glance, as she sorted through the bundle of mail, looking for anything that might be hers. The young man turned to look at her.

"Are you a tenant here?" he asked her, his manner curt and abrupt. Taken aback by the brisk tone, she stopped and looked directly at him. Only then did she notice the stripes on the overalls that told her unquestionably, that this was the Police. Forensics was an obvious, with the overalls replacing the standard Uniform.

"Yes," she replied hesitantly. "Why? What's happened?" she asked, slowly walking towards the car he was leaning over.

He continued his brushing, looking her up and down with focused intent, as he went on with the job at hand.

Coming closer, she could now see the great slashes making up words cut deep into the windscreen. The long scratches all over the bonnet of the usually immaculate Mercedes.

"Do you know what mammon means?" he asked, taking her by surprise with this strange query, ignoring her question.

She had been leaning over his shoulder reading what she could, the daughter's names, first, second and last names, a few 'fucking's', 'mammon' and some other dribble she could not quite make out, and at a guess from the way they were tending, did not want to make out.

"Whoa, I'd better not touch anything, hey!" pulling back when she realised she was leaning on the car as she bent over, trying to read what was there. "No, I don't! Is it an abbreviation for mammoth or something like that?" she continued, answering his, now not so strange, question.

She had seen this word a few months before, when someone had done the same thing to the big glass double sliding doors of the little Office, but she did not offer this information.

She knew it was something he would already know about from the last time they attended, so she chose not to admit to any knowledge of either event, not wanting to involve herself in their investigations in any way, shape, or form. This was definitely one of those times where taking sides was irksome to her. With neither parties stroking any of her loyalty strings enough, to lure her from her own welcome and private world.

The young Policeman, saying nothing, just watched her in that alert way.

"Do you know anyone with a glass cutter?" again ignoring her question, he asked her in a more casual manner, still dusting as he went.

"No. When did this happen?" she was asking as a couple of other tenants, who had been on their way out, paused to have a look.

"Last night," the young Policeman said, finally choosing to answer her question and then immediately dismissing her in the same casual manner. With that alert look in his eyes, he asked the other two tenants if they knew what mammon meant.

She took the opportunity to quickly move on, saying, "Well, good luck" as she walked away, not expecting any answer and not getting one.

The place was crawling with Police for a few days. You'd have thought the local Bank, or some such, had been robbed.

She knew they had always had their nightly drive-throughs. She also knew they did this just to let all the tenants know they were keeping an eye on them, and she could understand this, with the amount of drunken, drugged and just pissed off people she had seen about, up to all sorts of no good, once the sun went down. Zombie haven, to be sure.

She did not answer the door at night, mainly to save herself the bother of contending with the swaying, slobbering creature that was looking for company, for whatever reason.

She knew, that while they gave this special attention to the Complex, and was, to some degree, because the owners were of such a great age and in need of a little back-up, she still could not help but feel that the Koins, with their long levity in the area and their ownership of a good deal of property, carried a great deal of clout with the local Authorities.

Having chatted with a few of the young Officers who drove through from time to time, she knew they all knew of Mrs Koins dispensation towards confiscating property and the putting on the street of tenants she would rather have gone, all the while claiming they were behind in rent. She had seen her come up with four different set of figures for the same tenant once, for what was supposedly owed. Complaints to Authorities were common, yet no one ever did anything or even spoke to her about it. It was a general attitude amongst the young local Police that, "That's old Mrs Koin for you" (yeah, yeah, and yeah), and they would tell any complainers, "You have to take it to Court." That, their hands were tied because it was now, 'out of their jurisdiction.'

It was more than a few of the local landlords who used this by-line to the Tenancy Act. Some, even overlooking the giving out of weekly receipts in order to support their ambiguous claims, should ever the need arise. The tenants, not having a leg to stand on then, and chided that they should have asked for, or kept, their receipts, and that it was thoughtless to have not insisted on obtaining them, in the first place. Trust, in this situation was never advised, and ultimately, the problem one of your own making.

Once the verbal claim was made to the Police, after an unwitting tenant had tried to get their property back, that they had owed money to the landlord, all the Police could do was direct the tenant to take it to Court, the dispute, now having to be solved by Court intervention. A long, arduous and expensive process, few ever did, preferring to simply abandon their belongings and move on, a lesson well learnt, instead.

She had not been home long, after quickly slipping away from the industrious Forensics Officer, when Alexander had come over. He had been watching out for anyone who was out and about, and she had been the lucky one.

Sitting at the big wooden table outside, he had asked her if she had heard about what had happened. A big smile on his face, he was obviously enjoying the thought of what a great expense of fixing a Mercedes in such a condition, would be for the owner. He told her they had been questioning everyone and he was staying out of their way. After all, he was not a likely candidate to offer any help to the Koins, he said, laughing. "Let the bitch stew in it!" he had declared.

"Happened in the middle of the night, they said," still smiling, he continued, "No good looking at me, you know I can't walk without my walking stick, and you know the noise the metal tip makes, hey?" not quite a question, he grinned deviously at her.

She noticed his skin, even more pallid than usual, had droplets of sweat about to run down his unwashed face. His thick rattail hair, greasier and in array. He looked as if he had not slept for a while, and she could smell the red wine that had stained his mouth, about him. She had to make a conscious effort not to screw her nose up, at the combined aromas floating around him.

"Let alone bending over to do all that, my old back isn't up to that!" he stated, leading the conversation where he wanted, pointedly directing it for her.

"Must be the same person that did the doors, though. Good on them, I say!" he went on enthusiastically, congratulating the perpetrator.

She watched him, listening to the levity in his voice. When she still said nothing, he continued persistently.

"Can't stand that woman, in her tight stretch little shorts all the time, dripping in all those gold bracelets and rings," he said, referring to the daughter with these often repeated, time-worn, slurs.

"Never did a dam thing for me in all these years. You see my front door is almost falling over. The gap under the door gets bigger and bigger, I can see peoples' feet when they knock!" and on, and on he went, belligerent now, a childish pout forming about his stained lips, determinedly trying to win her over to his side.

She let him take all the time he wanted on this day, killing two birds with one stone. You could not always say you have no time to chat, and he was a wealth of knowledge on what the latest was, when something like this was about. At times such as this, with Police coming and going everywhere, it was good to know what the latest was. One of those deployed, self-survival things, it was good to know what was what, when trouble was about in your own environment.

She'd had the feeling at the time that Alexander had wanted to tell her something, to tell her more. Something had shifted. His manner had become inviting, as if he wanted her to question him in some way, but she had dismissed it, not wanting to spend any energy or give any commitment to something that she really did not care about, and definitely did not want to become involved in.

Darn good thing, as it turned out.

Alexander had a close friend he had known for a long time, who would come and get him for a late night wander together. With her walking beside his old-fashioned motorised chair, hands thrust into the pockets of her work shorts, going uptown to stare at the glamorous and noisy crowds out for a night of gaiety.

They would point and laugh together, at the foreign and untouchable alien breeds around them, speculating on which ones would survive the night and which ones would not.

She had finally moved into the Complex a few months before the attack on the Mercedes, after her flatmate, unconscionably, became engaged and left her high and dry, with an expensive rent she could no longer afford alone, and so, it had become a case of, 'hit the road, jack!' for her. She was a self-declared gay lady. Questionably so, because she was dammed unfriendly to all the females about her, and it was not an uncommon way to fend off unwanted male attention by claiming to be gay. The men also, seemed to treat them more as one of the boys, ensuring their safety and acceptance, and giving them the freedom to come and go, unimpeded.

He had bought an unwitting Annette a fancy new mobile phone as soon as she had moved in, and they had subsequently, had the usual massive falling out, with her screaming at him late one night that she had to start work early the next morning.

She was a cleaner at one of the Hi-rise Holiday Apartment blocks, and it was a job she valued greatly. Lateness, was completely out of the question to her. She had been known to defend her sleep often. Once, when her next door neighbour was still playing Religious videos, on maximum volume, at two in the morning, during a break between them, she had managed to get her message across by yelling at them to "put God to bed for fucksake, would you!?" Bringing a smile to everyone else's face within earshot, and to those especially, who had been thinking the same thing at the time but reluctant to say anything. For a moment, she was hero to the sleepless around her.

After exacting his payment for the phone, everyone at home that night heard how Annette was going to shove Alexanders' bloody phone up his arse any minute now, if he didn't piss off with his foul texts to her. The image this threat brought to mind, made the nuisance of it all, well worth it.

She had often thought that sending crude texts was Alexander's way of getting off, same way as some do with dirty talk phone calls. What else could induce such an expensive outlay for otherwise little reward, she questioned.

It must have been a beauty of a text or two, because Annette was still not speaking to him weeks later, and she was happy to tell all and sundry about 'the dammed moron,' she used to call a friend.

She was sitting with Annette and a couple of others at an outdoor table, one morning not long after the assault on the Mercedes, when Mr and Mrs Koins' daughter had walked down the driveway from the Office, looking around to see who was outside and watching, she came directly to their table. She leant over Annette after excusing herself to everyone, and she softly said, "The Police are up at the Office, they didn't want to come down here and single you out in front of anyone. Would you come up to the Office and tell them what you've told us?" The question hung in the air.

"Sure. You go and I'll give it five minutes or so, then I'll come up," Annette said quickly, as if doing so would get it over with sooner.

Waiting for the daughter to walk away before turning back to the small group sitting with her, she was silent for a few moments. She sat, rolling her coffee cup between both hands and looking at her feet, finally, she answered her companions' silent questions.

"Alexander told me he did this, and they have been focussing their attention on the young girl who was visiting with Simon that night," she said in a whisper, excusing herself to this unwanted and unwelcome audience to the previous proceedings.

"Didn't seem right to let her take the blame for it. Bloody moron!" she continued in her own defence, glancing over her shoulder at the closed door of Alexanders' unit.

"I knew it was him when the big doors were done, anyway," she paused, "because, I'm the one who first told him of the word 'mammon,' and what it meant!" She smiled sheepishly at everyone sitting around her.

"I didn't know he would do something like this!" she said, more a statement of innocence than anything else.

Putting down her mug, she shrugged, stood, and walked toward the driveway leading to the Office.

The small group watched her go. Her head bowed. Her tall frame and long thin legs accentuated by the perpetual shorts and gym boots, with the rolled down football socks, she always wore. Her hands shoved constantly, and boyishly, into her pockets.

They looked from one to the other, no one wanting to be the first to say something, then all of them talking at once.

In mutual agreement, they decided it was going to get interesting at any moment now and everyone was staying put, just to see what unfolded next. After all, they all had a vested interest of some kind, in seeing Alexanders' comeuppance finally hitting home, and this was an unforgiving mob at the very best of times.

Expectantly, keeping an eye on the driveway leading from the Office, they all watched the closed, rotting door to Alexanders' unit, as if already seeing the Boys in Blue standing there.

Time ticked by, and seemed to the little group waiting expectantly, to take hours and hours to pass.

Ten minutes later, two young Policemen walked down the driveway, nodding to the group as they went past. They glanced at those others watching out of windows and those coming to stand in open doorways, proudly displaying their contempt for Alexander and his plight. Not even trying to hide themselves away now.

They continued on, to stand before Alexander's door.

PAUL

Finally, some weeks earlier, unable to cope anymore with the tiny Motel room, she had taken on a larger, more expensive unit two doors down, and Buff her Protector, was now three doors away.

She had given up on keeping tabs on the movement of people through the unit next to hers. Must be the Ley Lines governing that particular place, or something. It had been an unending this one in, that one out, another lot out, and so on, and so forth. Ley Lines maybe, but she suspected it was more about them being particularly too loud, particularly too much the nuisance, and then to top it off, too much of the, 'Oh, the rent can wait.'

While the Koins overlooked most of the goings on because they had to, there was not a quiet character in the place and the Complex would have been empty otherwise, they did not overlook unpaid or late rent. Never given any grace for lateness, it was one of those things Mrs Koin could not understand and she often stated aloud, her inability to fathom how anyone could not make sure the rent was taken care of before all other things. It never occurred to her that circumstances could leave the pot empty on the rare odd occasion, and the back paying of overdue rent was something accorded to a very few long term tenants, and only once even then. They would pay the price of any such oversights in budgeting by being shown the door, as far as Mrs Koin was concerned.

First there had been another young couple with another female who swore like a burnt out old bushie who had spent life in the outback, under the sun, around the campfire and cattle. Their tenancy had gone the way of the 'kicked out' when, after a rip-roaring dual punch up with each other, culminating in a huge black eye for her and the young man packing his kit up and taking off, leaving her to pay the extravagant rent on her own. Stranded, it did not take long to show her inability to do so. She had managed to pick up a young man or two here and there, the sound of noisy smacking kisses heard easily through the paper thin walls between units, but they had not lasted longer than the intended night. Finally, when she had to admit defeat, and at the insistence of Mr and Mrs Koin, after such a loud and look at me stay, she left quietly without any fanfare, and unnoticed by most.

Then, there had been a young fellow who had been placed there, after much beseeching to the Koins, who finally yielded in their opposition to him when challenged, diplomatically, on their Christian values by one of the charities who helped the homeless young addicts get off the streets. Except this young addict came from a wealthy, well to do, family. With three other highly successful brothers to contend with, he performed with finesse, the art of 'Up Yours!' purposefully going against everything that his sad but understanding, newly remarried father, ran around trying to do for him. If he felt they had not been quite attentive enough of late, he would find something outrageous to do that would put him before the Courts again, the situation demanding another rescue, and that would be the families 'what for!' looked after once more, until the next time.

He often wandered around after the sun had gone down, knocking on the doors of the single women in the Complex, who, after mistakenly opening the door to him, were only caught out the once though. Once, was more than enough.

He would be full of prescribed Valium and half a bottle of Vodka. Wearing only a loose pair of shorts, he would put his foot in the bottom of the open door so it could not be closed, then, he would pull his shorts down to expose himself to the unwitting female, who would by this, be yelling for help from whomever could hear her wails and telling the young man to, "bugger off!" in very animated and loud ways, a few of them even landing an adequate closed fist, to his jaw. Until his endeavours became well known, and had been experienced at least the once by all of the women, this had been an evening ritual for the first few weeks of his tenancy.

At one of those times, our Dan across the way came dashing over and with one king hit, dropped the young man where he stood. After laying him out flat on the crumbling concrete driveway, he stepped over the motionless figure as he headed towards home, mumbling to himself about the annoying little turd, all the way back to his waiting wife.

Eventually, he stopped paying rent and also was shown the way out. Much to the relief of the single women there, who had also begun to ignore him in his habit of sneaking up to their back bathroom windows looking for cracks to watch them through, when he could get away with it. The neighbouring males looking out for him, after one of them had caught him at it and given him the thrashing of his lifetime.

His father and the disapproving new wife, bringing the trailer and loading up his belongings while he drunkenly watched on, one arm slung around a supporting pole of the carport to hold himself up, and the other cradling his opened, half empty bottle of vodka. But not before he had managed to re-invent his unit by changing a few of the walls around and ripping up all of the carpets.

A quiet, middle aged fellow came after that, one day just appearing from nowhere. He sat daily, outside the front of the unit in a big old chair, having nothing to say to anyone but not bothering anyone either. He always had a blanket wrapped around himself, and word spread that he was dying of some sort of cancer. It was one of those rumours that just started making the rounds, no one knew how it began but it picked up pace quickly, and surprisingly, all of the tenants gave him gentle consideration.

He had moved in because he did not want his family to contend with this part of it, and he wanted to spend the last moments on his own, or so they said. Everyone was polite to him and they left him to himself, only calling a distant hello to him as they passed by. It was only a matter of weeks when one day, one of the girls living on the other side of the fellows' unit came tentatively asking, if someone shouldn't break his door down. She had no hot water, and she was sure his shower had been going since the day before. Sure, she could hear it through her bathroom wall. She had knocked and knocked on his door, to no avail. Someone went up to the Office and came back with the spare keys, after earning the right to confront the Koins on the loss of a tossed coin.

They found him on the floor of the still running shower, and he had passed away sometime the day before. The sad little group watched the blinking lights of the ambulance as it turned onto the main road, taking any proof of the mans' existence with it, and leaving the observers with a chilling reminder of their own tenuous hold on life. No one even seemed to know what his name had been.

It was a very young couple that moved in after this. The girl was only eighteen, and he was barely a few years older than her. He was different though. Different from any others there. You knew they were all dangerous in their way, street wise and beyond. He was somehow more intense, more closed off, more in a world where he was fighting some great battle and it was only him against them all, and his life would be forfeit if he slipped, just once.

His overly tall, spindly frame was undermined by the stooped, rounded shoulders as he slouched his way along. Hands shoved deep into his pockets. Head down, staring at his feet, only looking up at you through the fringe of the shoulder length, stringy blonde hair which danced and bounced about his head as he walked. He never spoke as he passed by. The scowl on his lips a warning to others, and a protection against any who might try to engage him in casual conversation.

Mrs Koin had asked her to keep an eye on the girl, since she was only eighteen and her neighbour. Mrs Koin had also told the girl, if she should need assistance with anything, to seek her female neighbour out.

Hmmm … she had thought, when told of this. Especially since her ruling code was to keep to herself and involve herself in naught. The Three Monkeys had been invented for a place such as this, she was positive of that. Still, she had daughters around the girls' age, so it was true, she had a concerned place in her heart for one such as this girl and she would probably have kept a helpful eye out anyway, so she had said nothing about the overly generous offer that had been made on her behalf. This was a place she would never want to see her own girls staying in. A bit of a contradiction, since she was on such an adventure herself, but that was parenthood for you. The old adage of 'do as I say, not do as I do,' was something that all parents practised at one time or another, it came with the territory, and she made no apologies for it.

It was not long before she knew the lass was in over her head. She stopped and listened the first time she heard the loud bangs and crashes as furniture was misplaced and thrown about. Not thinking the girl was in trouble the first few times she heard it, only wondering at the often moving furniture. When she began to hear the muffled grunts as the girl tried not to cry out when he punched her, alerting the neighbours to her plight, she started taking more notice and began to watch this one more carefully, to take a look at him as he came and went, albeit, a look on the sly but a look nonetheless.

She knew the truth of it when one night early, around seven o'clock, the little lass came tapping quietly on her door, imploring her to open it quickly. The girl stepped inside, hurriedly closing the door behind her, half collapsing and leaning back on it to steady herself. With no explanation, she begged her to hide her, to "shush, be quiet, don't let him know I'm here!"

The girl was frantic in her panic. It was then that she took her first real good look at this wisp of a very young girl. Thin and tiny boned. Barely reaching the age of womanhood. To look at her, a good wind would blow her away. She wondered how such a tiny creature could withstand the onslaught of the tall young mans' constant anger, and his physical expressions of it. Wondered, after what she had already been listening to, how bad had it become to send this girl running, frantic and frightened, to the door of an unfamiliar neighbour, seeking her protection?

With whispers and reassurances, her arm around the girls' tiny waist, she sat with her on the end of the bed. Remaining still and just holding her, she let the little girl take her own time.

Gently encouraging her to breathe deeply, telling her she was not going to let him near her, the lass began to calm, the shaking in her tiny frame starting to slow. With words tumbling one over the other, in hushed tones and making no sense at all, she tried to tell her story. The tears rolling in floods down her cheeks, leaving shiny tracks as they went. You could tell she was frightened by what may be coming, but this time, she did not appear to be hurt physically, not that you could see, anyway. It seemed she had managed to predict the trouble to come, and had ran beforehand.

There was no knock at her door, or yelling to come out, everything was silent. There was no noise from next door, no thumping or banging things around, no movement anywhere. It appeared the young man had not yet decided to follow her. Either that, or he had not yet realised the lass had ran so close by, to a relative strangers door, instead of running out onto the street.

She knew she was not going to be of any real help if this fellow did discover where his girl was hiding. That any defence she could offer, would only really come in the form of bravado, but she did not say any of this out aloud. Knowing from the experiences of her years, that sometimes, coming from a stranger, standing up to him might work short term, it would not work long term. No, not at all! It would only serve to mark her for the future, when he would be there, waiting. Still, she could not abandon this girl and live with herself if she did, anyway. The risk was hers alone, and she knew she had to take it.

She had seen his type many times before. Cowards, in truth! Standover a woman and cower from a man, but if ever they marked you, they were as dangerous and determined, as hell. She knew what she was going to do. Grabbing the young girl by her wrists, she gently pulled her to her feet, with one arm around her waist to help support her, she moved her towards the locked and barred door. Saying in hushed tones, "Don't worry, we are going to get some help."

"I'm taking you over to Dan and his family. I'm sure he will protect you, at least he will know what to do. No one will come near you over there!" she explained gently to the still fidgeting, frightened girl, who was having trouble getting her legs to support her, she kept sagging at the knees.

Exhausted, instead of the protesting she had expected, the girl only nodded her head, tears still rolling down her face, her lank long hair in disarray. She clung tightly to her, her tiny hands surprisingly strong in their firm grasp on her.

Opening the door as quietly as she could, she poked her head out for a quick look around the enclosing darkness. First off, only taking enough time to make sure there was no one she could see hiding behind the huge old Palm trees running the centre of the driveway. She had decided to go quickly, with no hesitation. The time honoured 'just make a run for it'.

It was almost like holding your breath and closing your eyes, then waiting to see what grabs you. Urging haste to the lagging girl, her arm still around her tiny waist to hold her up, she half pulled, half pushed her towards Dan's unit on the opposite side. Stumbling and tripping on the loose and broken bits of driveway as they fumbled their way through the darkness. Catching her breath when they passed the great Palm trees where you could never be sure someone was not hiding and would be well concealed. Feeling sick, she was aware of the butterflies flying about her stomach. This was something akin to going up those dark stairs in any horror movie. The "No, don't do it!" kind.

Making it safely to the door, she didn't get quite the response from our Dan across the way that she was hoping for, or indeed, had expected, with his past tendency to champion besieged women.

After a lecture from him about being on a Good Behaviour Bond with the Courts, and many a 'how can I get involved in a potential punch up?' and lots of 'Bloody Hell's' for good measure, a quick glance at his unusually quiet wife's face, he took the girl in.

She excused herself, telling the lass she would be safe there now, and wanting to extricate herself from the situation as quickly as she could, she covertly made her way back home, taking the same route as before, and with the same amount of caution. The lights were still blazing in the young mans' unit. All was silent, but with her skin crawling, she thought she could feel eyes on her now.

Breathing a great sigh of relief as she closed her door behind her, leaning back, her own legs failing her finally, feeling wobbly, she double checked the security chains on her door before she could relax and look for the air that she seemed to be having so much trouble finding. At least she would not appear to be a meddler to the young man and the girl, for the moment, was alright and in safer hands than hers could be.

Dan made the best decision possible, only at the insistence of his wife, she was certain of that. He phoned the Police, and as against the grain as it may have been for him, wisdom had won out for a change. They came, they talked with the girl, who told them her story, and then they went and spoke for some time with the tall young man, who was totally innocent and somehow misunderstood.

They went back to the girl they had left at Dan's unit and they told her they could do no more for her unless she would press charges and of course, she was not prepared to do this. His already recorded past infringements would not have withstood such new charges, and the retribution that would come from her involving the Police was something she would not chance.

After giving the young man a stern and genuinely meant warning about what would happen if they had to come back again, they left. The girl eventually, went home. And that was that.

The lass never spoke to her again, pretending not to see her when she passed by, only moving to the other side of the street. She knew this was embarrassment from a very young, inexperienced person, and she did not hold it against her, but she also knew that the periodic beatings and temper tantrums still continued. The girl never asked for her protection again, fearing interference from the Police or the threatened consequences such actions would bring her way this time, either way, she was content to be left out of it now, and she did not seek the young lass out in any way, not wanting to make things any worse for her.

Only, the next person the tall, broody young man took on wore more than a few raps from the baseball bat that was used to belt him with.

Paul had moved into the unit on the other side of her and he had a sweet and jovial disposition, in direct opposition to the tall young mans' sullen and moody ways. She often felt she was like a neutral territory, stuck between the two opposing forces.

Paul was no angel though. While he worked full time as a bricklayer on a new Estate in the City, after hours he was a big time dealer of grass, but he was also a content young man of around thirty, without any predisposed aggression anywhere and a serious side you had to dig deep for. In grandmothers' day, he would have been called a Good time Charlie, easy going and popular with everyone. He spent a good deal of his off hours having a few ales, and he was happily pissed most of his free time. Earning good money from his day job, the expensive fast car he drove could easily be explained, if needs be, because of this regular high income. Not that this concerned him, sensible caution over his exploits was a casualty to his happy and carefree ways, and could not be found applying anywhere in his interactions with other people.

She had noticed that the broody young man had begun to visit with Paul and could be seen over there often, playing the unfamiliar amicable scallywag with him, and always drawing the attention of those around watching who knew different. She had no problem condemning the young man with the thought that his friendly attentions to Paul were provoked by his interest in the grass Paul always had in abundance, and his generous and pliable nature towards everyone. They would sit together on the table top, their legs dangling over the side of the rickety wooden outdoor setting in front of Pauls' unit, laughing and drinking from the cans of cold beer they held. Paul, calling out to her laughingly, as she came from or went to her work, always had something cheery to say to her. The brooding young man ignored her at these times, keeping his eyes on his swinging feet and not looking up at her.

She saw the glares he threw her way when she glanced back over her shoulder, on these occasions. He made sure she knew he did not hold the same friendly thoughts for her that he displayed towards Paul. The help she had given to his girlfriend weeks before would not be forgotten, she also knew to be true. Not even trying to give him the benefit of the doubt anymore, in those glares he gave her and the warnings they delivered.

Integrating himself bit by bit, he began to ask Paul to drive him places, telling him he would put up the petrol money and Paul being so agreeable, generally did this for him. They appeared, to all those who noticed, to be getting rather close.

She knew a few of the people who lived close or opposite had begun to watch this kindling friendship. Those, who had only distant encounters but still doubting his motives and curious to the fact that the broody young man continued to ignore all of them, with not a word or a smile for anyone and his scowls still offered up in abundance, knew there was trouble coming. The Complex being what it was, everyone had heard of the time the Police had come to rescue the girlfriend from the young mans' fists.

The one thing that stood out to her at these times was the absence of the young lass, who was never with him on these visits. He would saunter over, a six pack in hand and never any excuses offered for his missing girlfriend. And, she could feel the storm brewing and the thunderheads gathering. The undercurrents which always accompanied the broody young man were a defining thing, a black cloud following him everywhere.

One evening on twilight, some weeks later, she heard yelling from just outside her unit. Lifting her curtain back just enough to look outside, she saw a very drunk Paul, swaying, hands supporting himself, leaning on the top of the outdoor table to stop himself from falling over, and the tall, broody young man, a baseball bat in one hand, threateningly pointing it at Paul.

She was glad she had not yet turned her lights on.

"Open the door, man!" he screeched at Paul.

"I got piddling all, man. It wasn't enough!" the young man told him, pointing at Paul with the bat, while suddenly seeming to realise something. He had looked furtively around, keeping his voice low now, trying not to attract too much unwanted attention, it had sounded like a forceful hiss.

Paul, telling him in a wailing, repetitive roll, "I can't get in, my girlfriend has the keys!"

He tried desperately to keep the table between them, fending and compensating the young mans' movements off. They looked like a couple of kids playing Chase around a playground full of obstacles, only the raised bat hinting at any menace.

"What do you want me to do? I can't get in," Paul, still repeating again and again in a drunken slur but it fell on deaf ears. His pursuer, with focus, was intent on him only.

She knew then, in an instant, that the tall young man had waited his opportunity, that he had no intentions of an amicable outcome, and that he would not be talked down. Paul was in trouble.

She looked around and saw that all the lights were off, except at Dan's unit. The Complex looked deserted tonight, only a few lights on in the units towards the back, at the far end of the driveway.

"Open the door!" the young man demanded a little too loudly again as he began to move around the table towards Paul, trying to distract him with his words, relying on his impaired responses to fail him now.

Paul, continually retreating, trying to keep distance between them, stumbling and almost falling at times, he was going to lose the protection of the table at any moment. If he went down, he would not get back up again. The young man was waiting for just such a thing, ready to pounce. Enjoying the hunt, his bearing was that of a stalker intent on his prey.

He was after Pauls' stash and she knew now he meant business, there would be no happy endings. He was sober, calm and calculating, and it was clear, unless Paul got help from some other quarter, he was not going to get out of this in one piece. The awaited time had now come, and the Hunter would have his way.

The young man had coveted the car Paul drove, and Paul's apparent unending supply of money while he was unemployed. The conversations that had drifted her way over the last few weeks on those drunken, noisy afternoons they shared together, had told her this already. He begrudged having to pay for the petrol when he had a lift somewhere, the cans of beer he had to offer up as his share, and Paul's happy disposition, he begrudged the most of all.

So, he had waited his chance and nothing was going to save Paul a good flogging, even if he did 'open the door.' This fellow was out to punish, and he was going to have his pound of flesh. His intentions surrounded him like a dark cloak, the moving energy was almost visible.

The darkness had fallen, twilight was gone. The huge Palm trees were the usual black sentinels, waving their arms in the slight breeze as if threateningly waving off any intruders but unable now to offer any solace to the distraught Paul.

She continued to watch, somehow not wanting to leave Paul alone in his peril. She wondered how many others were doing the same as her, from the darkness of their units. As she looked around the Complex, she knew it would be more than just a few. There were some who would be talking quietly to each other on their mobiles, close enough in their friendships to be sharing this dark moment. And, she could imagine the way these conversations might be going, with more of the "Don't get involved man, you know better than that," than any other kind of advice. It was the way of these people, survival and self-protection would be their only thought.

There would be more than a few of them, who thought that Paul might have put himself in this position. That he was not so blameless, in his own downfall. There were some who had been waiting for this. Maybe not such a brutal turn, but something. She was not the only one who had seen that cloak of darkness every time the younger man was about.

Past experience told her that no one would interfere with this kind of confrontation. Self-survival was the only priority, and in this kind of situation, in a place like this, you were on your own.

Especially, if you did not have the sympathy of the population, they could be hard in their judgements. Besides, they expected you to know this and to look out for yourself, that, to involve them, was downright inhospitable and inconsiderate. But, it was also true, they could be kind and genuinely supporting to an innocent victim, and as staunch as all get-out.

She felt sad for Paul. And, it was dead right, he had walked straight into this situation. Flaunting his money, booze, fancy car, good job and plenty of dope, around people who had little of everything, including food. With most of their money going in rent to keep a roof over their heads, it had been a bad move, if not madness.

He should have seen it coming. In fact, he should have had a better strategy than party central, if he was to prosper in these environments. Only, she truly believed that his genuine innocence was to blame. An inability to spot the dangerous jealousy, but this was going to be a lesson he could never forget, and lost innocence would be the price paid.

He had thoughtlessly made himself into a target. A big, round target painted on his back, and he had, unwittingly, made friends with maybe the most threatening character in the whole Complex.

He was chasing Paul now. Having manoeuvred him away from the table, it was Palm tree to Palm tree. Paul, with nowhere to hide, heading for the only visible light, was trying to make his way towards Dan's unit. Unable to watch where he was going for fear of taking his eyes of his pursuer, tripping over his own feet here and there, but somehow, not going down.

The yelling, becoming one constant scream, was rising in pitch. The desperation was hard to ignore. The broody young man, eager to get this done before anyone tried to stop him, no longer saying anything, only stared madly, eyes fixed on Paul.

And, unconcerned now for the noises around him, only intent on his purpose, was closing in fast.

In the darkness, it was becoming harder for her to see, but she knew from the pitch of the screams, that Paul had taken a few direct hits from the bat.

Dan had come outside and was standing, hands on his hips, in front of his door. The lights behind him making him easy to see, but he made no move to intervene, only watched the dancing pair.

Feeling sick in her stomach, her eyes darting around, looking for a kind rescuer to miraculously appear, she noticed that the lights in the back units had gone out too. The Complex was still and in complete darkness, as if everyone had suddenly vanished. A hushed silence had fallen like a pall. Except for Dan's place, where the lights still glowed. She saw that he was saying something to the broody young man but could not make out what it was, the screaming too loud to hear anything else. The young man, not missing a step or averting his attention as he answered Dan, was now moving like a stalking cat.

She could imagine it was something like, "he ripped me off!" She guessed this would be familiar and understood ground, something very few would get between.

Dan went back inside his unit, closing the door behind him, but the lights stayed on.

Finally, losing his struggle to stay upright, Paul was on the ground now, the young man standing over him, looming like some imposing black shadow.

She saw him position the bat above Paul's head. Instead of taking a swing, he just let it drop onto Paul, and she knew from the way the scream cut off midstream, it had connected hard. The young man stepped back, lifted the bat and swung hard at Paul's thigh.

The screams rose once again in pitch, multiplying as they did. Paul tried to roll awkwardly away from the descending bat.

She could hear sirens in the distance. Someone had called the Police.

Probably Dan. Not intending to offer any involvement himself but taking pity on the drunken fool on the ground, who had not made any effort to defend himself. The grog, taking away his ability to gauge the seriousness of the situation he was in as well, until it was too late.

No one was ever sure who had called them.

Sirens blaring, warning other travellers of the swiftness of their insistent journey, but also warning everyone of their impending presence and giving the scoundrels their opportunity for escape or concealment. Safety for the majority was the greater priority. Even so, a more sedate and stealthy journey perhaps reaping a more successful outcome, than a prior warning for the perpetrators to seek out their escapes, might do.

Sure enough, the broody young man lifted his head listening to the sirens drawing closer and closer, then, after a half-hearted kick towards his torso, quickly walked away from the prostrate form of Paul, still rolling slightly from side to side. He reached his own unit, went in and closed the door. She heard the loud thumps and bumps against her adjoining lounge room wall as he threw the baseball bat up and over his wardrobe, where it settled with a clatter, on the floor behind it.

Two Patrol cars drove into the side entrance, spotlights settling on Paul, now lying still and unmoving on the pitted, broken ground. Blood covered his head and smeared down his naked chest.

Swiftly, the four Officers went straight to tend to the beaten and bloodied Paul, before the Ambulance arrived not far behind them. Pulling up beside the Patrol cars, orange flashes showing the bent and crouched group, working on the lifeless and unmoving form on the ground.

All of the lights in the Complex remained off, with doors closed and curtains drawn. But, she could feel everyone watching, that familiar knotted feeling you get when walking alone down a dark alley told her she was not really alone here, at all. The Ambulance Attendants laboured over Paul, finally lifting him onto a stretcher and moving him to the Ambulance. She saw two of the Officers talking to him, while the other two spoke to Dan, having had to knock loudly and repeatedly on his door before he would open it and come outside. She saw Dan shake his head now and then, shrug his shoulders pointing this way, then that. At last, going back inside and closing the door with a final loud bang.

When no one came to knock on the broody young man's door, when the Ambulance and Police cars had left, she knew then that no one, including Paul, had been prepared to tell the Police what had really happened that night. Even Dan would be ambiguous in his story. That was no surprise, more to be expected, than not. Dan's lack of love for anything to do with the Authorities was a well-known fact, and he would not choose to involve himself, no matter what the cause. Turning his back on the whole affair as soon as he was able, the safety and security of his little family coming first and his only real concern.

The Police knew what had gone on, that was a given. But, unless someone pressed Charges or told their story, they could do nothing more than pick up the pieces afterwards.

She guessed Paul had been reluctant to tell, not to protect the young man, but to protect himself. He was more concerned for the huge territory in which he dealt grass and them discovering this, than he was for dobbing the mongrel with the bat.

Paul would not forget the beating he had taken, or the betrayal of the friendship he had offered, and this was not going to be the end of it. Not by a long shot, no! He had decided he would handle it his own way, just as soon as he was fit enough and able bodied, once again. The louse would pay his dues, Paul was determined about that. And, he would do it the only way that gave him any real joy.

The tenants never knew the extent of Pauls' injuries, but since he had been speaking to the Police as he lay on the stretcher in the back of the Ambulance, they all assumed he had survived the attack. Positive that they would have all been approached otherwise, the lack of Police interest to be seen around the Complex since the beating was confirmation of his survival, as well.

No one, except Dan, ever spoke to her about what happened that night, and even he assumed she had not been home at the time. She never corrected him or hinted that she had seen it all, only let him tell her his story, quietly nodding along with him as he went on with it.

It was a funny thing, gossip of the small kind would spread around the Complex lightning fast, but with something like this, no one ever admitted to knowing, or having seen anything. Self-protection was one of those commonly shared and respected things, uniting the strangest of bed-fellows. She smiled at the irony of this truth.

She did notice that everyone took the long way around the broody young man when they unexpectedly came across him, and no one looked his way anymore.

Even the Koins, who periodically pumped their tenants for gossip on any questionable activities they thought might be going on, like, 'why do so many visitors come and go from that unit?' and they did not mind singling someone out to have an informative conversation with, never said a word to anyone about what happened that night. No questions were asked, not a one.

They could not have missed it, the screams ringing out, and their little cottage only up the side driveway and so close by. Thinking about it, it was likely they who had phoned the Police. She could not imagine them ignoring the screams on hearing them. If so, they had been uncharacteristically quiet since the affair had happened. Surprisingly, the degree of violence involved this time might have quieted more than just the tenants, maybe.

It was common place for them to call the Police for the slightest little thing. Not to mention the evening drive-throughs that were a permanent service and which never seemed to happen when something was actually going on, much to the relief of the young Officers on duty, she was sure.

It was about three or four weeks later before anyone saw Paul at the Complex again.

About ten o'clock one night she heard a low hum, the engine noise of a car, slowly driving into the side driveway and pulling up right in front of her unit. Alerted by the stealthy sound, she knew she was not expecting anyone. Taking particular notice this time as well, because no lights had flashed across her front windows. Unsettled, and unsure of what had caused the noise, getting up, she moved to the window and lifted the edge of the curtain to take a look outside.

In the darkness, against the rising moon, she could make out the figures of five men getting out of the darkened car. One, she recognised was Paul. Wearing only a pair of jeans, even his feet were bare. He swayed slightly and she knew they had filled up on some Dutch courage before embarking on this covert little mission.

For all their stealthy entry into the Complex, Paul moved around to the front of the unit next door to her, lifted one hand and hurled a beer bottle straight at one of the large glass windows, shattering it with a loud booming crash.

Yelling, "Come out, you mongrel coward!" "Come on, let's see how brave you are now, you fucking arsehole coward!" he slurred, his voice cracking and hoarse.

The other men stood around Paul, all of them silent, watching. Retribution was at hand.

The whole group had something in their hands. Some had bottles, some had lumps of wood. Paul took another bottle off one of them and threw it at the other window. The resounding crash echoed off the units opposite to sound louder than it really was. Still, the men were motionless. Immobile black figures, silhouetted against the rising moon. It was a disturbing and threatening sight.

There was no movement from the unit next door. No lights went on. No sounds could be heard.

Sirens in the distance grew louder and louder, making no mistake of their destination. They were coming fast this time.

The smart young man had called the Police rather than taking the group on. He had not given any hint that they were home, and luckily for them, they had turned their lights out and gone to bed earlier than what had seemed to be their usual habit.

They already had the spotlights on and glaring as they turned into the driveway, tyres screeching they came to a sudden halt. Three Police cars carrying six Officers, lights swirling, sirens blaring, making a hell of a racket as they had come.

The other men with Paul mobilised quickly and they scattered in different directions. All of them running, but not Paul. The spotlights framing him perfectly. Standing there, bare chested, his bare feet with no shoes on, and a great long carving knife in his hand.

The glaring lights showing the healing cuts on his head and the yellowing bruises on his body, a testament to his previous run-in. He was a gruesome sight. And, made all the worse to look at by the long carving knife firmly gripped in one hand, he was a successful spectre to any midnight revenge.

Two of the Officers had taken off running after a couple of the sprinting men, while the other four all drew their guns and aimed them straight at Paul. They surrounded him quickly.

Yelling at him, "Drop the knife, get on the ground!"

Paul just stood there, sometimes swaying in some sort of intimate dance, for what seemed a very long time. Their loud demands to drop the knife and get on the ground becoming more and more imperative, the message urgent and their intentions clear.

The now silent orange swirling lights, tracking orange beams around and around, lighting here, now there, and taking in all of the adjoining units surrounding the group of people. The orange glow contrasting against the dark night and the constant glare of the fixed spotlights. The four Police Officers, motionless, with their pointed guns aimed at the slightly swaying figure of Paul, all of it looked so surreal. A dreamlike moment, frozen, framed against the pitch black of the night.

She held her breath.

She knew these modern young Officers didn't muck around, and that if he made one wrong move, they would take him out.

Paul seemed to become aware they were there, squinting into the glare of the spotlights and looking dazedly around at them as if he did not recognise where he was, or who they were.

He slowly let the knife fall to the ground.

They were on top of him fast, pushing him into the concrete, knees on his back, twisting his arms behind him. They cuffed him and then lifted him in one swift movement to his feet.

Two of the Officers taking him to one of the Patrol cars, leant him over the bonnet as they roughly felt around his jeans pockets. Paul, leaning on the bonnet, looked around bemused and muddled, shaking his head slowly as if to clear it, or in disbelief of his well-planned and awaited payback having been snatched from him.

The other two Officers, now searching the area with torches, had already bagged the great carving knife. The swinging lights of the searching torches, back and forth, adding to the confusion of the swirling orange glow.

All of the other running men got away. Judging by the pace they had taken off with, they had not been as Dutch courage up'd as Paul had been, their escape swift and sure footed, each choosing their own route to freedom.

Being such a small seaside holiday Resort Town, all of the young Officers would have recognised, or known of Paul from the beating he had taken three or four weeks earlier. The ones who had attended then were possibly and most likely, amongst these six Officers.

They also would have been unsympathetic, if not annoyed, with him for not pressing Charges or even telling them what had occurred when he had the chance to. They would be especially hard on him for taking vengeful matters into his own hands no matter what, and by now, they would have put two and two together, to what was really going on here.

While one of the Officers stood talking to a handcuffed Paul who was now sitting in the back seat of the Patrol car, another knocked on the door of the unit next door. The internal lights of the unit, now on, showing the youthful face of the Officer clearly, as he waited for the occupant to appear.

The other four Officers were standing around the driveway, in what she recognised as a loose semi-circle. Appearing relaxed, a hand on a hip, one leaning more on one foot than the other, and one standing only a few feet or so away, right in front of her own darkened doorway.

She could have reached out and touched the young female Officer, her hair in a tight bun that poked out from under her cap. She could see the flicking of her tightened jaw, the only give away to her tenseness, her eyes intent on her fellow Officer standing almost casually, still waiting for the unit door to open.

She could not help herself. Maybe it was the injustice of it all. Of what she knew was coming for Paul. Knowing these Officers had no choice in the Book they were going to have to throw at him because of his own stupidity, and his lack of backbone in pressing Charges in the first place. She knew it did not matter what these young men and women thought about it, their job was merely to enforce the Law, not agree or disagree with it. He was going to wear jail time over this one, and the most dangerous one of all would walk away, unscathed. So, she broke her Cardinal Rule.

She opened her door just a crack, whispering at the same time so as not to alarm the already tense and alert young woman standing there, almost casually.

"He has a baseball bat behind his wardrobe!"

The Officer did not even glance her way. She just bobbed her head ever so slightly. Nothing in her stance giving anything away, her eyes remained riveted on the closed door and her waiting partner.

She quickly shut her door again as she heard the creak of her neighbour's door opening. They spent some time speaking with the broody young man, asking the same questions in different ways, over and over. But, he kept them at the door, lounging against the doorframe as he spoke.

No, he did not know why he had been singled out by the group of marauding and malicious men, maybe it had been a case of mistaken identity.

No, he didn't know any of the men who had come to attack him in such a vicious way.

No, he did not own a baseball bat.

The kid was savvy, and game, she had to give him that. The Police could not search his unit without a Warrant, and he stuck to his story no matter how they twisted the questions around, remaining as relaxed and helpful as any innocent man might do. The girl, quiet for the most part and only mumbling an uncomfortable "No" when they asked her any awkward questions, telling them often how frightened she had been by the whole ordeal.

Paul, having been hit with a Restraining Order amongst all the other Charges, including Intent to Cause Fear, never returned to the Complex again.

His girlfriend, coming with some friends to pack his belongings up and take them away, never spoke to anyone, and she quietly and efficiently went on her way, pulling her loaded up trailer behind her. She had watched her sadly for a while, knowing what the happy, boisterous Paul had ahead of him, and that his life would never be what it had been, ever again.

Talk about shooting yourself in the foot. An understatement, when it came to Paul.

As before, no one spoke of what had happened that night. The young couple next door disappeared sometime after, seeming to just fade into the ether.

WILLIAM

William was an odd-one-out but fitting in at the same time. He was an older man, over sixty but not yet the sixty five that he needed to be, to claim retirement and the Old Age Pension. He came from the generation where Superannuation had not existed through his working life, and he now discovered he was too old, and unwanted by the majority of employers. Unable to live on the pittance offered by Unemployment Benefits, it was an untenable situation.

Caught out by the unaffordable rents like so many of his age group, with no workable solutions, he was stuck between a rock and a very hard place. He was a clever man though, and he had worked out his own way of dealing with the System that had put him in such a hopeless position.

In his younger working days he had been the Marketing Manager of a very large and well-known International Company, so he was no dumb bunny, and he was accustomed to finding the needed solution to any problem. He had travelled the world in his work and the diversity of standards and living conditions he had seen through these times, stood him in good stead to cope with the uncomfortable and unpleasant living conditions he now found himself in.

He had chosen to come to Koins Motel after the Boarding House he had been living in, had put their prices up to such a level as to be downright annoying to him. The only difference was, his previous abode included meals, but he had worked that out, too. He had a plan for everything he did, his years spent as an organiser was now a way of life, taking very little thought for him and applied easily, and effortlessly.

She first met William when, one evening on twilight, she had turned a corner into the driveway leading towards the Office and had the scare of her life, had in fact, nearly had heart failure.

In the fading light, coming towards her was a figure clad head to toes in white. A strange apparition, in his white shirt, white shorts, long white socks, and with white grey hair. His arms outstretched to shoulder height to warn him of any bushes looming in his path, or to alert him when he was about to walk into any shrubbery on either side of the driveway, or to tell him that he had wandered off his allotted pathway. Whatever the reason, he was a white spectre in the gloom.

There he came, floating down the driveway, the perfect ghostly vision. In the twilight he did not realise she was there until he was almost upon her. The thick glasses he wore did not seem to give him any real aid, either.

After asking him, "What the bloody hell are you doing?" and him stating, "Avoiding the bushes!" he told her he was new there, and he pointed out which unit was his. His ruddy cheeks, a contrast to all the white and belying the good health his rotund frame suggested. A rotund figure made all the rounder by the shortness of his stature. As an apology for the scare of her life, he invited her for coffee when it suited her and she said she would be sure to come over sometime, only going on her way after he had convinced her he didn't need any of her help to get himself home.

"The practise is good for me!" he told her cheerfully.

He was a short, tubby, tidy man with cropped grey, going on almost completely white, hair. He had a slight South African accent, left over from young days and giving away to those with a keen ear, his place of Birth. He had inherited the unit opposite her and right next door to Alexander after it was vacated by a disgruntled and 'had enough of all this shit,' Rita.

Her final straw had come in the form of a very angry, long term tenant who had a grievance with her and did not mind sharing it about as expressively as she felt was warranted. Vanessa, who was a single mum to an active young son also had a raging, years' old speed addiction and her level of patience with outsiders was zero. When Vanessa had been told that Rita had said something to someone about her, and her volatility being what it was as a consequence of the years of injecting herself with Speed, she had dashed down to Rita's unit, blustering all the way.

"I'm not copping this shit from any bitch around here!" she muttered to herself, her legs and arms working in unison as she rushed, unthinkingly, toward Rita's unit.

Upon seeing Rita, Vanessa marched straight up to her, gave her a substantial loud slap across the face screaming at her at the same time to, "Stop talking about me you whore, or I'll kill you!"

She spluttered at her, "You don't know me, you fucker, OK!?"

Spinning on her heels, she stormed off just as promptly as she had arrived, still muttering to herself, arms flapping back and forth, all the way back home.

Rita might have been able to contend with the slap, even the threat, but she could not deal with everyone in the Complex having a good laugh about it. Especially, since their laughter was open and unhidden, and their mirth sprung to their grinning lips every time they saw her.

Rita was in fact, more than deserved of this type of accusation, and everyone was happy to assume she was guilty as charged. It was enjoyed by so many who had felt a kinship for Vanessa over that moment of reprisal, that it became the talk of the Complex for weeks later, and was a welcomed jovial pause in a usually unhappy and sullen environment.

William had moved in less than a week after Rita had moved out with the help of a 'happy to see her out of this dump' ex-husband, who was still reeling from Alexanders' graphic revelations. Neither, saying anything to anyone as they drove out of the Complex, only letting everyone know of their last minute disdain by the glares they delivered as they went by.

She next saw William a few weeks after meeting his now well-known, arms outstretched apparition coming down the driveway. Everyone, with the exception of a very few, had lived through their own turn at this extraordinary experience. It was at one of the Sunday Services she had been asked especially, to attend. Since the old family friend who generally came to help out, had decided to do a dummy spit of monumental proportions after Mr Koin told her that her grandson would not be saved. Because he did not pray daily on his bended knees, because he did not say he believed in Jesus, that was it, he could not be helped. She had hurried out, and she had not been seen since. But, Mr Koin was unrepentant. He saw nothing wrong with telling her the truth. Her young grandson was not a believer in Jesus and he was therefore, going to be doomed. And, Mr Koin could not see it any other way.

She was late to arrive and everyone was already sitting in their positions opposite each other, Bibles in hand and open, ready for whatever Reading was chosen for that day. Feeling self-conscious, she moved quickly to a vacant chair, murmuring her apologies to everyone whose knees she knocked or feet she tripped over. Settling down as quickly as she could, she saw her chair was placed directly opposite Williams'.

She was about to offer him a smile of acknowledgement when it struck her as she sat down, the way William had looked her up and down. Taking in her hair, her dress, and then her shoes, and in that order. Then, he had continued his appraisal by staring at her. Without any real thought, she was instantly aware that his scrutiny through those thick black rimmed glasses was clearer and more direct than it had been that twilight evening, when they had first met on the driveway. With amusement, she thought she might watch this one closely, all of a sudden not believing his story of being legally blind.

Now that she had noticed this scrutiny, she saw even his glasses looked like they did not really fit, were a bit too large, and they slid around somewhat. Their frames were cracked and chipped, giving the impression of being very old and already well used.

She had found it funny when Mrs Koin had previously remarked, quite casually, that he did not have any trouble reading which ones had been his mail, from the communal mailbox in the Office wall.

She had laughed to herself at the time, thinking, "Good old Mrs Koin, she sure misses nothing!"

Over the next few months, she had morning coffee now and then with him, but after that encounter at the Sunday Service she always had trouble stifling her amusement at his, almost, but not quite, perfect presentation of a legally blind person. Sitting at the table outside his unit, she had been content to go over and see him on those occasions when coffee was loudly suggested, yelling across at each other with the driveways and great Palm trees between them, and as always, preferring not to have anyone come visit at her unit, or at least, whenever she could manage to avoid it.

While she knew he was a bit of a scammer, even so, the story he told of how his eyes had become so bad was quite bizarre. Of how, the Specialists could not say what was truly wrong with them. He was nevertheless, a good conversationalist. Telling her all sorts of tales about his young life in South Africa and his many stories of the time he was Sales Manager of such a large International Company. His pride showing in the cheery way he animated his tales, bringing them to life for her, and taking her away for a time, from the solemn and challenging surroundings they both lived in.

He continued to attend the Sunday Services because that was his meal for a Sunday, and she would often see him making his lonely ethereal journey, with arms outstretched, up the driveway to the little Chapel called Deliverance Hall. He never pressed her to join him in this journey, accepting her decision to decline, and she was grateful for this.

His other days were sorted from a combination of events by differing Charities. Two nights at the barbeque held in the local Park, not only for the homeless but for anyone who wanted to come and share a spiritual conversation together. Another two nights for sandwiches handed out by enthusiastic young people volunteering their time to an honourable cause, and delivered kerbside, from another charity's travelling food van. All of it meant he had no need to ever cook for himself in his own unit, which he never did, his fridge remaining gladly empty.

You would know what day of the week it was by the time of evening that he went off, arms extended ahead of him, to meet his dinner. She had to admire his organisational skills, and he remained as tubby and rotund as when he first had arrived.

She also smiled at William's constant catch-cry of, "Sorry, I can't see anything!"

Whether someone had asked if he had seen someone go past yet, or what time did his neighbour leave for work, it did not matter what. Even if he had said hello to the neighbour on his way out, it was still going to be, "Sorry, I can't see anything!" His cheeks growing redder, the flush rising with his sometimes awkward, denials.

Most, had stopped asking him such silly questions. And, he had done his job well, for there were some who even replied for him, "No good asking him, he can't see anything!"

Everyone by this, had seen his familiar round figure standing outside of his front door, doing all his strange eye exercises, including 'going around the clock', all given to him to practise by his Eye Specialist of course, and used to support any claims he made. Only a few could be heard now and then, calling to him as they went past with, "What the bloody hell are you up to, William?" sometimes followed by a, "You look like a bloody goog, mate!"

He was to be sorely tested in his control of the 'I can't see anything,' and to those who were not watching closely, distracted by the unfolding events, he came through with flying colours.

The morning had been eventful, beginning with a distraught William looking for aid from any of his neighbours who might be about or close at hand. He had a calamity he needed some assistance with, which he could just tell, was going to be a big deal for him.

Telling them, there was dirt or something, coming up through the drain hole in the floor of his shower, and he, being unable to see clearly what was going on, could they please come and check it out for him? By the time it was all over, everyone within yelling distance had been in the see what was going on in Williams' bathroom.

The shower was a mess. Brown muck all over the floor and up the walls. The smell was something to be reckoned with, and immediately suggested the identity of the brown sludge as soon as you walked through the doorway of the little room.

Someone, taking pity on him and his lack of agility, went up to the Office, saving William his difficult trek, and the Plumber was called in. After numerous inspection holes were accessed around the yard behind the unit block, it was finally decided that the problem had been years in the making, and now, the job would be rather large and untidy, as roots from the big old trees out back had cracked all the sewerage pipes. It was raw sewerage coming up through the shower drains, and would have impacted on the other units too, given a little more time. In a way, Williams' mishap had saved any others from a similar fate, warning of the trouble before it gotten out of hand.

Raw sewerage was something that had been a bit of an obvious but hoped not, by most of those who had stuck their head into the shower stall that morning. A few of the women dashing back out with hands cupped over their mouths, and a good deal of dry retching and cursing to go with it.

It was going to turn out to be a much bigger job even then, than had first been suspected. It went on for over a few weeks and ended up affecting every unit along that side of the Complex. The tenants involved taking showers anywhere they could, some relying on just the surf to do its' fine job, and all of them using toilets which were offered up by generous neighbours. Everyone spent most of their time hanging about outside, the shocking smell impossible to tolerate, permeated everywhere and everything.

A few hours later on that first morning, the Plumber having done what he could until the heavy equipment arrived the following day and everyone else happily and a little thankfully, disappearing again to leave William with it, realising there was not much they could do anymore anyway, she had suggested that they should stay outside with a big hot cuppa.

They were sitting together having their coffee and idly chatting about nothing in particular, when the tenant in the unit on the other side of William came ambling out, looking relaxed and unperturbed by the smell engulfing his unit. Getting into his newly acquired bomb of a car, slamming the door and turning the engine on, he continued to sit there for some time, loudly revving it. Taking the time to rub the invisible dust off the dashboard with his hand before reversing out with a scream of the tyres and barrelling down the bumpy and uneven side driveway, he lifted a hand in slight acknowledgement to them as he sailed past.

They watched him on his way, shaking their heads but saying nothing to each other. Giving it little thought, they went on enjoying their coffee and conversation with some relief after the horrible, smelly morning that had left them feeling dirty all over.

Half an hour later, the same tenant drove back in, repeating the whole process again. Finally, screaming to a last minute halt in front of his doorway. They were about to pass some chiding comment to him as he hauled himself out of his new car but before they could do more than open their mouths, Dan across the way, threw his door open so hard it bounced off the outside wall, almost swinging back to hit him in the face. He put a hand out to steady it as he stormed through the doorway, taking long strides toward the tenant. Coming quickly, pointing his finger at him, he yelled, "I'm sick of you! You fucking arsehole! I've told you before to stop tearing around here, what if my little girl was outside!?"

Without pause, he grabbed the frozen fellow by the shirt front, swung him around so severely the material ripped, clutching onto it as the tenant fell heavily to his knees onto the concrete driveway. Dan, keeping his hold on him dragged him to his feet, smashing him backwards into the glass front door of his own unit. The crashing sounds of glass breaking and flying around, and the smaller pieces tinkling lightly as they landed on the bitumen. The thunderous tones reverberating under the outdoor awnings like the distant rumbling of a storm.

They both sat fixed to the spot, not daring to move in case they got in the way of a very angry Dan and ended up as collateral damage, with themselves splattered over the concrete driveway alongside the stunned and unsuspecting tenant, who was lying splayed out and face down on the concrete where Dan had let him drop. Glass scattered all around him, while Dan, still yelling and cursing at him was already striding back towards his own unit and the small toddler watching him from the open door.

Fumbling with the smaller pieces of glass all over his chest and belly and having little success with it, the tenant dazedly, pushed himself slowly to his feet. His shirt ripped down the front exposing long, flat, flopping breasts, telling of a time in his life when he had been a victim of obesity. Small bleeding cuts and scratches covered his chest and arms, with a few long cuts towards the top of his forehead just below his hairline. The blood, slowly running down his face and dripping onto his ripped T-shirt and bare chest, making him appear grim in the shadows of the overhead awning.

"I'm calling the Police, you mongrel," he yelled shakily after Dan.

"Don't worry, so am I!" Dan stuck his head out the door, waving the phone he already had in his hand.

William, unthinkingly, put a protective hand over hers. Otherwise unmoving they both still sat frozen with mouths open, watching all that was unfolding so quickly around them. They looked at each other, not daring to move anymore than the slight shifting of their heads, then as one, looked back at the progressing drama.

The tenant seemed to find his thoughts. Still cursing and spluttering to himself, he got into his car, reversed it out at a more sedate speed and drove it up to one of the back units. Parking in an empty carport he got out, locked the door and began his walk back down towards his own unit again. Muttering his threats and profanities as he came, stumbling over the pitted ground, his bloodied ripped and torn visage looking for all the world, like just another zombie coming for his vengeance.

Finally finding her voice she whispered to William, "What is he doing?" And with little hesitation, still watching the approaching figure, William replied, "Hiding his car."

Before she could ask, "Why?," Dan came back outside, regarding them purposefully.

Walking over to the table they sat at he said pointedly, "Now, when the Police come I want you to tell them you saw him slip on the concrete." He had one hand resting on the table and he leaned over it slightly, watching them sternly.

"OK?!!" his tone not reflecting a question asked, rather, supporting the demand he had just made.

"I can't see anything, it's no good them asking me," William said, stumbling over the words as he was apt to do when nerves were at play, anxiously trying to convince Dan of his authenticity.

"Okay! Just make sure that's all you say!" Dan told him, eyebrows raised, the warning clear. William bobbed his head in consent. Dan looked at her in turn. Seeing her enthusiastically nodding her head at him, he gave her a slight nod and turned back to go and stand in his open door, awaiting the arrival of the expected Police.

The Patrol car was just driving into the side driveway as the tenant, on his way back from parking his car, passed them sitting at the table. Ignoring them as if they were not there as he continued on, to go and meet the approaching squad car.

The two Officers sat in the idling car for a few minutes, listening to what the excited tenant had to say, taking in the cuts and dripping blood, the ripped clothing, before the driver lifted a hand towards him requesting he wait there. After parking the Police car, the two Officers, walking back towards the bleeding and dishevelled tenant, motioned him to join them to one side as they approached him. Glancing over to Dan who was still standing in his doorway watching, his little toddler cradled in his arms, they told him, "You stay there, don't go anywhere!"

"Why would I?"

"It was me who phoned you!" he called back to them, sounding almost casual and just a little sarcastic, implying that he had priority here, since he had made the phone call.

Both of them, pretending to still be interested in their cups of now cold coffee and trying to be nonchalant and disinterested, could hear quite clearly the stories being told to the two uniformed men. William seemed unaware he still had hold of her hand.

After making their way towards Dan's open doorway and the man standing there, waiting, with the child cradled on his hip, held there like a shield against the approaching men, one of the Policemen asked him how the tenants' shirt had been ripped if he had just slipped on the broken and cracked concrete. Dan, without hesitation, confidently said he had put his hand out to stabilise the fellow as he was going down, catching hold of his shirt, it had ripped as a consequence of this offered aid.

Making no effort to approach their table, the Policeman had looked over towards the pair of them enjoying their coffee and called out loudly, "Did he slip?"

To which William answered quickly, his hand still resting protectively over hers tightened slightly, "I only heard it, I can't see, I'm almost totally blind. Sorry, I can't help any more than that."

She only nodded her head, not trusting her voice. Watching her, the Policeman paused before turning his attention back to Dan and the little girl he was still holding.

She breathed a sigh of relief. For a moment she had thought he would push his questioning, placing her in a precarious position. Not a place she wanted to be, where Dan was concerned.

When Dan told of the complaint he had regarding this fellows' hooning, they forgot their interest in whether he had slipped or not. Turning their attention to the tenant, they changed direction entirely. Discovering that the offending bomb was now parked up at the back units, they ran their usual checks. Finding that, not only was it unregistered but their Records showed the driver was also unlicensed, and with a few pending and unpaid Fines still collecting, bringing slow grins that were hard to hide, to the youthful faces of the two Officers.

After sorting their way through the only details that now seemed to interest them, they put the tenant into the back of the Squad car and drove him back to the Station. Much to the tenants' chagrin, who, finally acknowledging them, showed his displeasure to the two figures still sitting at the outdoor table, by sticking a finger up at them from the backseat of the car as it turned onto the main roadway and disappeared. Leaving a satisfied Dan to smile and nod his thanks at them, as he went back inside and closed his door, promptly dismissing the whole matter.

They charged the hooning tenant for all sorts of things including drug use once they had tested his blood levels for both alcohol and narcotics. Keeping him overnight in the cells and not releasing him until he had made his Court appearance the following morning.

Well, Dan had a win, finally. Rewarded, for standing his ground this time.

CHRISTMAS

The warm salty sea breezes in the evenings eased the high summer heat of the days, a welcome respite, and making life a little easier for coastal residents than it was for those living inland. Christmas in Queensland was always a muggy, torrid affair with humid storms regularly ending each day, and the torrential rain raising steam off the hot bitumen roads, a cleansing sauna provided by Mother Nature for all to enjoy. She loved the smell of the rising steam caused by the heat of the bitumen and the cooling rain, the way moisture dripped off the green tropical plants everywhere and the freshness of the air after each storm.

Everything seemed to slow down at this time of the year as if turned to slow motion by the flick of a switch on a mechanical device. The days were long and lazy, the people just as layback, and the demands of the season itself, seeming to ease people into the holiday weeks of the Christmas period.

While she wondered at the joy of what a winter white Christmas must be like in Europe, and she could only imagine how beautiful it must be with all of the old traditional Festivities appreciated by all, she nonetheless loved this time of the year in Australia. Beautiful decorations spanned the length of the main street with great colourful loops strewn high across the roads, and every shop window showing off their own lovely Christmas scenes. Santa Claus was on every corner, and the sounds of his ringing bells filled the air.

The happy, laughing, boisterous children dragging tired arms' laden mums around the shopping centres were filled with expectant delight at all they saw. Their excitement contagious to the most cynical of watchers, encouraging the involvement of everyone they saw.

Every Club, RSL and Pub had continuous Shows and Revues running, heralding the Festive Season for all to enjoy and crowds spilled out onto the streets with regularity every night, stimulated to continue their onward journeys by the louder and gaudier Club next door or down the street.

A few of the home-bodies, the ones who had no family to go to, had decided that to pool some money for tucker would be a good idea, and that to join each other for a communal Christmas Day lunch would be a nice thing to do. Making everyone feel like it was Christmas for them, too.

Well, you know what they say about good intentions.

The evening before Christmas Day, just after the sun had gone down, she had wandered outside with a coffee and a rollie cigarette to sit quietly on her own, on the table top of her outside table.

It had become her habit to do so in the last few weeks, since the Local Council had erected a massive shining Star atop the great Bunya tree in the Park opposite Koins Motel. When she had first seen it towering up there, looming over the whole Complex, her immediate thought had been, "How about that! Even Koins gets Christmas. Well, well! Some things can't be held at bay, even in this God forsaken place." Enjoying the taste and warmth of her coffee and the solitude of a now almost emptied Complex, with most having deserted the place for the comforts of an annually rediscovered, 'Oh, that's right! We have family somewhere!' she sat, feeling comfortable with herself and the time of year.

She watched the grand Star above her head, swaying ever so slightly in the gentle breeze coming off the ocean. The great moon was a perfect back drop to the lovely Star. Tiny glittering twinkles here and there, surrounding it. Her heart lifting at the significance of how this moment was her Christmas present from The Great Out There, the Divine if you like, and she felt her gratitude by sending a small thank you to them, for the timely reminder.

She intended to put in an appearance for the lunch tomorrow. What she did not know yet, was that lunch would, somehow, end up being laid out on the table in front of her unit and the putting in an appearance, would turn into an afternoon slog at her expense with people traipsing in and out, to use her toilet and bathroom and whatever else they thought they were entitled to.

The morning, beginning quietly enough, gradually picked up speed after Annette came to her door with an armful of the things they had gone together to purchase (cold meats, pre-made salads, Christmas cake and some sugared fruits, all from the pooled money), and dumped them in an untidy pile onto her outdoor table. She had left them with Annette in the first place, in order to distance herself from the laying out of a Christmas lunch, but those intentions now going out the window. A good beginning to what the tone of the day would be.

She slurred something like, "you sort it, be back later." There was no Merry Christmas though, and throwing her a blurry eyed glare, with head down she ambled away, feet scuffing the ground as she slouched her way along in her usual long strides, shoulders working back and forth in time to her mincing hips. A forlorn vision on this universally cheery morning.

It took only one look to realise she was totally off her face on grass, and like so many others who spent Christmas on their own, was pissed off at the whole day in general. Best to just overlook it with an, 'I've noticed nothing' attitude, but she knew it would only get worse as the day progressed, and on past experience, with people who suffer from this kind of dislike, if alcohol is added to the mix they were usually not great to be around.

William was the first to come across. Having left it until a civilised time of morning and deciding it was lonely on his own and too bad, if he was going to be the first one there. He sat at the table chatting about nothing and being generally jolly. She saw that he had come empty handed, but who would know since he was the first to arrive, and everyone knew he didn't drink at all, anymore. She doubted that anyone would even think of it, let alone care, if they did. Besides, most had already put their dollars' worth into the kitty and would presume, so had William.

By lunchtime, a dozen or so stood around with their chosen drinks in hand, some talking amongst themselves, others animating noisily back and forth to each other, content to be doing something different for the day other than the hard slog their usual workloads demanded.

William, happily smiling at everyone, occasionally glancing in the direction of a sullen Annette, who, now nursing a Jim Beam rum and coke, sat beside him, eyes swollen and red, glaring into her drink as if it was wanting in some way. Annette, resolutely determined in her continued anger, only looked up once to watch and curse under her breath toward a lone Alexander, who appeared down the main driveway, dressed in a suit and tie and looking dapper and modern in his once a year clean-up. Tapping his way toward his unit, he took one look in her direction and decided it was not a good idea to join them. With another unhappy glance toward the gathered group, her scowl encouraging him in his homeward journey, and her offered animosity to be his only Christmas present. Miserably, he travelled on his measured way.

That breach not mended then.

They all noticed this subtle exchange and a few called out Merry Christmas to him, throwing amused glances at the sullen Annette. Others, unable to resist the temptation, laughingly flung taunts at him, never having seen this once a year clean-up before, and more than a little surprised it could be achieved at all, to which he lifted his free hand in friendly acknowledgement but he continued on without a rest, not looking back, only lifted hand waving his way onwards to his own doorway.

Sometime during the afternoon, when most had their fill of food and in rising high spirits had left for somewhere else they wanted to be, Janet came strolling around the side entrance and aimed straight at the three people, who were now the only ones still left sitting at the outdoor table. She strode up, plonked herself down heavily in a spot next to Annette, and after pushing the remnants of Christmas lunch to one side, asked loudly, "Who's got a spare drink?" she proceeded to take over what was left of this so far, fairly forgettable event.

She had never met Janet face to face, before. She knew that she was one half of the couple who had lived for a long time in the little cottage beside the main driveway, and were the only ones allowed their very own pet cat. An ancient and capable fur ball who rarely ventured outside, preferring to sit on the window sills, arrogantly watching the comings and goings of the less fortunate multitude that surrounded its' home grounds in abundance.

She had no idea about the man Janet shared with, only that he was about twenty years younger than her, putting him at about forty five, and that they had been together for a good many years. She suspected this union was one of mutual convenience in shared expenses, him, appearing to be a gay man and her, an ex-Showgirl, or something of similar ilk.

She was about sixty five, but kept herself in good nick. Her bleached blond hair always swept up in a glamorous pile atop her head. She still got around daily with her midriff showing, and from occasional observations now and then, she knew that Janet and her housemate often scored grass from their very local in-house dealer, also suggesting that their choice of any adequate surroundings took second place, in preference to more convenient and reliable connections.

"God, this is a rip roaring Happening, isn't it!" "What's wrong with you?" she threw at Annette.

Before Annette could rouse her, very out of it by this, self, Janet continued on loudly after wiping her off with one quick glance. The malicious twist to her mouth said she understood clearly, what was wrong with Annette.

"Was gonna come over earlier but didn't like some of the arses that were here, and you know Peter, he didn't want to come at all! That's him, he never wants to go anywhere!" she said matter-of-factly, her practised excuse of putting the blame on him coming easy to her now. She was in Party mode, and happy at the sound of her own voice. Being the star of any Show suited her right down to the ground, and appeared to be comfortable and familiar territory.

"Who are you, you the blind man?" she threw at William, who sat smiling (and smitten) at her, his eyebrows raised and the interest showing all over his grinning face.

"And you are the good-looking one," he replied, never taking his eyes of Janet and still smiling broadly, his round red face growing redder.

She noted to herself that she must ask him how he knows that later, and then she followed this up with, maybe he is blind after all. She grinned broadly at herself, her own joke too entertaining to resist. Realising she was grinning, she ducked her head guiltily after having almost pulled off, she thought, a nearly perfect, innocent nonchalance. She wanted to grin again, but refrained. A quick glance around reassuring her that no one in this little group had eyes enough for her, to have noticed this indiscretion.

While Janet presented herself well and was still physically taut, the skin on her well used, sixty five year old face was flabby and sagging, and when she spoke her lips gave the impression they were flapping up and down. It made it hard to look straight at her, left somehow uncomfortably trying not to stare, and being somewhat unsuccessful at it, finding your eyes always drawn to this intriguing phenomenon. She felt the urge to giggle again but managed to stifle it before it became too apparent to the audience around her. Oh, the fun she was suddenly having!

Clutching her stubby of beer in her hand, Janet stood up and walked, hips swaying, midriff bare, around to where she could sit directly in front of William, singling him out. Her intentions clear from the twinkle in her eyes. Saying, "Us old bod's should stick together darling, don't you think?" smiling at him seductively, in appreciation and more than a little gratitude, for his compliment to her.

Hmmm. So, no one else noticed the contradiction of "are you the blind man?" and the "and you're the good-looking one," except her, hey? It didn't surprise her. Annette, probably not hearing anything by this, was in a very out of it world of her own, and Williams' timing for such slips had always seemed to be good, so far.

She also noticed, the woman had not directed any acknowledgement toward her, or taken any notice of the fact they had not yet met, either. She simply was not there. Totally invisible. She wished she could learn this trick herself, it would make the flapping lips easier to bear. And, so typically females from another generation long past, their weapon of choice, the Obvious Snub!

After the tiresome morning of wasted conversations and enforced running about, she decided it was a blessing in disguise and would let the lady have her way. Choosing to sit quietly with her Christmas glass of wine, which having been poured for quite some time was now becoming bitterer with each sip. Not forcing her own way in, or making any form of protest, or trying for any one-upmanship, she contented herself with watching the people around her, always a favourite pastime to fill an empty minute or two.

"When I was a younger woman and working the Nite Clubs in Sydney, I met a lot of arses. I can tell you a story or two." Still, Janet appeared to be speaking only to William, her concession for his obvious interest in her. Flirting with every movement she made. Him, loving every second of the rare attention now coming his way. Her eyes dancing mischievously, touching his hand lightly here and there, leaning towards him, making good use of the angle of the table top she rested one arm on, to lift her breasts enough to show a little cleavage or lifting her free arm in a stretch that hinted at the bottom of her breast, which would soon show below the edge of the tiny top which exposed her midriff. Every slinky move was a well-practiced performance, and all of it for him.

Oh well! If anyone knew all the tricks it had to be an old Showgirl, she was sure. And this one reeked of being in charge of all of her moments.

"I got one of those arses a beauty once," she continued, with the confidant air of a story told many times over and now known by rote. Not waiting for anything more than a nod in response from a still grinning, eyes locked, William. Satisfied, she went on with her tale.

"He thought he could push me around, strong-arm me, hey! When all his charm and good looks didn't get him his way with me," she laughed, enjoying herself thoroughly.

"You don't Fuuuck with me!" she said, a little too enthusiastically, a warning offered in the way her eyes flew quickly around the little group sitting, listening.

"I'll get them, you bet, every time!" "Bloody wog bastard," her eyes now looking thoughtfully into the distance, a well-chosen pause, then going on, "Or maybe Lebanese, or something like that."

She took a mouthful from the bottle in her hand and absentmindedly looked down at it, in unintended appreciation for its' cold comfort and familiar contents.

"Dripping in bloody gold anyway, whatever he was!" she declared.

The silence hung heavy in the air for a moment. William was riveted by the story already, and her attention to him held him like a frozen mouse in a snakes gaze.

Oh, she's good, this one. Knows how to play to a crowd that's for sure, she thought. And, for a crowd of one, she added to herself laughingly. She was beginning to enjoy the performance.

"Anyway, thought he was a big man around town, he did!"

She went on, "I was supposed to fall all over him. He thought!" she smiled, looking down at her kneecaps, head tilted at just the right angle, as if she was a coy young girl.

"One night, I'd had enough of the creep, so I invited him home with me," a small smile playing on her lips, turning them upwards at the corners and appearing more like a forced grimace.

"Only, not to my home. I took him to a Hotel. Not that bloody stupid!" she checked quickly to see if she still had Williams' rapt attention. She did.

"An expensive, ritzy City Hotel, mind you," and as an afterthought she added, "made him pay for it before we went upstairs, too! What a silly bastard!" She laughed loudly.

Annette, now leaning heavily on the table top with both arms, head drooping closer and closer on its' downward journey towards her arms, looked bleary eyed and disinterested. The rum and coke doing its' job nicely to top off the multitude of grass she had smoked since early morning.

Someone is going to pass out soon, she thought, with a another spontaneous grin at the comical appearance Annette now offered, in her determined attempt to miss the whole day.

"I made sure I had all the toys I would need with me," a big smile on her face, the grimace now gone. The lips still flapping, up and down, up and down.

"After a bit of a cuddle up, I made him take all of his clothes off!" she stated, short and sharp.

Getting the reaction she wanted as Williams' smile slipped slightly, much to Janet's appreciation of his keen and continued interest. She knew she had him hooked, by his unmoving silence.

"The poor, silly bastard. A man and his cock, hey?" grinning happily, she took another big mouthful of the disappearing beer.

"Anyway, I tied him up to the bed but not spread right out. I cuffed his hands to the bedhead," her waving hands emphasizing the how of it.

"Then, I used a soft rope around his ankles, bent his legs behind him and took the rope up around his neck," she paused, demonstrating to William how she had him leaning on his side to achieve what looked like, a very uncomfortable position to be in.

"You know what I did then?" she threw at William excitedly.

He almost shook his head, shocked, and too riveted to speak. Janet smiled and then, another mouthful of beer. Lowering her voice confidentially, "After I put tape over his mouth, I shoved a big dildo up his arse!" "Ha!" she finished. Laughing loudly, not wasting this moment, knowing she had her fish on the hook, she went on quickly.

"Got him a beauty, I did!" she had put her beer down and she reached out with one finger to stroke the back of a scandalized Williams' hand again. He jumped a little, as if he had been stung by something venomous.

"Know what then, my darling?" she asked, eyebrows raised and barely containing a smirk at the stunned look on Williams' face. It had been a long time since such an innocent as William had listened to this tale, and the solitary trip across the driveway was turning out to be quite worthwhile, for the demonstrative Janet.

Poor William. His smiled had slipped altogether but he still shook his head slightly, wanting to hear the end of this sordid and somewhat ugly tale, but also wanting to postpone it, too.

Janet glanced at Annette to see if any life had returned, but no, still no interest there. She shrugged dismissively, a little disappointed she was missing out on this performance.

Janet went on, almost flippantly now, "I left!" she said, flipping a hand over her shoulder.

"I just went and left him there!" she smiled sweetly at William, the coy young girl had returned.

"I admit, I was sorry I wouldn't see the Maids' reaction when she found him!" she took another big mouthful of her warming beer.

"Must've been a beauty!" she grinned, those lips a long slash across her face.

"Don't know how long he was there and," she paused, musing, "didn't care either!"

Finally, William found his voice, a frown crumpling his forehead, his common-sense showing, he asked, "Weren't you worried he would come after you, you know, sometime down the track or something?" His sincerity was genuine.

His keen tone giving away his belief that this really did happen. Or maybe, his horror at the thought of what if it had been him, not allowing him the opportunity to question the truth or validity of this story, yet. Certainly, his innocence, and up till now, reasonably clean living, leaving him ill equipped to spot a tall one. Even one as obvious as this.

Janet grinned at him, replying confidently, "Nup, I whispered in his ear before I left, he would find a very long knife in a very dark alley somewhere, if I ever saw him again!"

William sat in silence, just slowly shaking his head. Having forgotten to close his mouth and it now seemingly fixed, permanently open.

Annette's head had finally found her arms with a small thud, her near empty glass slipping out of her hand and spilling over. Janet glanced at her disgustedly.

As quickly as she had moved in and taken over the afternoon, Janet sculled the last of her warm beer, stood up and patting William on the head, said louder than was necessary, "Well, this is too dead for me, I'm off. Pleased to meet you, darlin," and she walked briskly away in the direction of her cottage, not looking back at them. There would be no curtain call.

Hips swaying in well-rehearsed motion, and humorously appearing to match the moving Palm fronds as she passed by them, with their dancing back and forth from the slight sea breeze coming off the distant ocean. A more comical sight than she would've appreciated, had she known.

Happy, having done well with this particular rendition of her practised tale, and glad of the newfound attention she was getting from a man. All of this, giving her the added bounce in her step.

It had certainly made Williams' day complete, as he still sat in dumb silence. Head turned to watch her go, in some way aware the Show was not quite over.

She never did get an acknowledgement. Not a nod. Not a glance. Nothing.

Well! That was Christmas at Koins for you. A story to suit the place itself, and nothing comparable likely to be repeated at any other Christmas' to come, making it memorable for this reason alone.

She had watched and listened, as was her designated role, and she was not altogether believing that this story was for Williams' benefit only.

She was not sure if it was a sad tribute to a young life lost, or a proud rendition of having been a Mover and Shaker, once.

Whatever it was, she'd had the classiest snub of her life, so far.

DAVANO THE IN-HOUSE DEALER

Sitting by the large open sliding windows in the front room of her little Motel unit, feeling the sweat run down her back between her shoulder blades and grateful for the breezes lifting the edge of the old curtains, she had been looking to find a cooler spot on this hot mid-Summer morning.

Trying to dismiss the musty smell the heat induced from the old carpet, a smell which seemed to stick in the nostrils and would not go away, she was finding it difficult to concentrate on the book in her hands, the heat sapping her energy and challenging her patience. It did not matter what she had done with the carpets, she could not completely rid them of the smell of years of abuse and lack of concern. Looking down at them now, their tattered threadbare condition, she would not be surprised to find inches of sand laying a cushioning bed beneath them, if they were ever ripped up. She turned back to the book she was reading, putting renewed effort into ignoring this constant and demanding distraction. Easily diverted, she had glanced up again when quietly muffled voices and scuffed steps had sounded near her unit.

Watching now, she saw the tall blond well-kept man she had first seen talking with Buff on the day of her arrival, so many months ago now. She had become accustomed to seeing him once a week or so, looking smart wearing his Boy Scout look-alike uniform, except that this had turned out to be a Coastal Volunteer Groups' Uniform. He often rode past on his boyish sized bicycle, with it squeaking it's way along. His tall frame overwhelming the smallish bike, like a tall man on a donkey might do. This combined with the uniform, giving the appearance from a distance of an exceptionally tall kid or overgrown teenager.

His shoulder length blond hair fluttering in the breeze supported this overall image that was only shattered when the lined and haggard forty something face, became clearer with the lessening of distance. His thin knobbly legs sprouting from below the above the knee long shorts, pumping madly up and down, as he went. The sight always induced laughter, and was cheap entertainment for all to enjoy.

All of this apparent community support and the pride he displayed in his uniform and membership, by the change in his already superior strut, contradicted the life he chose to lead in his personal time. He was an exceptional boozer. One, who could drink anyone under the table in his off hours, and he often proved this with any of the abundant amount of willing contestants who inhabited the Complex, along with those keen to stay in his good books. Especially, if they owed him money for any past purchases or wanted to reliably determine their future supply. To these people, it meant nothing to them to have to pat any egos.

They pampered and pandered to his every frame of mind and any stance of opinion. They let him rant and rave if he wanted to, nodding heads and agreeing with things they had not even listened to. They slapped his back, they laughed and they frowned. They ran his errands, they fetched his desires, and they pleased, however they could. He was King. And, he revelled in it.

With this kind of treatment having gone on, for God knows how many years now, his attitude toward mankind and his whole environment in general, was always one of self-assured arrogance and blatant self-importance. Everything he said and did, could hold no wrong.

He would talk down any rare dissenters, who might have challenged him on some topic while having a beer at the Pub or some other local haunt. Reason or accuracy had nothing to do with it, only that he held that particular opinion, and that should be good enough for everyone else too, he thought. His height allowing him to tower over most of his companions during these times, only encouraged him onwards, daring anyone to defy him. He would gladly tell all and any, how perfect he was and he often did just that.

His memory, his health, his skills, his knowledge, his principles, his schooling, all was perfect. He never forgot (unless he'd been too drunk at the time, but that did not count), he was never sick (unless it was a hangover or some flu, but that did not count), he was never turned down for a job (unless he was too old or something, but that did not count), he had been to the best school in Victoria (the best State School, but that did not count), and on it went. All of these conversations could be repeated verbatim by many of the regulars who hung about with him, having heard them all, many times before.

No one was ever going to break into his unit because he had surrounded it with an 'Energy' to protect it, and he was good at that too! No one had so far, after all!

He was a real gem. Unto himself, anyway.

On the days when his latest supplies had arrived, Davano would stroll from unit to unit. Standing outside, appearing as casual as he could, waiting for the door to open and the inhabitants to come out and join him in apparent idle conversation. Looking for the world like a weekly catch up only, where they would sit outside chatting for five or ten minutes, before he moved on to the next frequent and expectant customer.

On a few occasions, old Buff the Caretaker, spotting him on his weekly errands would join him for an inconvenient talk about general conditions and asking what he had been up to recently, as he walked alongside him, determined to just be a nuisance. After ten minutes or so, unable to come up with anything else to make delays about, Buff would amble away, a smile on his face and happy to have thrown a spanner into the works, but not quite prepared to openly challenge the younger man as to what he was doing out and about in the first place, in this weekly neighbourly pursuit, and always along the same old route with the same old people on the list of 'to do's'.

Coming back to the moment, she heard Buff, who was tinkering, head under the bonnet of some friends' car he was fixing in front of his unit, as he often did, give his usual unfriendly grunt in response to the compulsory 'hello' the men walking past had murmured towards him reverently, momentarily breaking their rapt conversation. She saw that the young man with Davano was the same fellow who could often be seen coming out of his unit after dark, to pee up against one of the big old Palm trees that ran up the centre of the driveway. She had no idea why he chose to do this, his own bathroom seeming to be closer, but the way he swayed at these times, often missing the tree altogether, spoke of how drunk he was, and she suspected it was just his way of saying 'Fuck You!' to the whole Complex.

Not brave enough to say it openly and this method, his second best choice.

She remembered the time she finally realised the role this Boy Scout played here in the Complex, and how silly she had felt over her gullibility and missing such a recognisable thing.

She had been aware of the vast amount of people coming and going from his unit, but had thought little of it, only noticing it was generally after hours or weekends. She had dismissed this to be anything of meaning at first, since she knew he went off to work every day and so, obviously, had to be after hours or weekends, it being the only time when they could catch up with him.

At first she had considered, maybe, they were hitting him up for a loan or trying to bum something from him since it was well known he had a good Job as a fibre-glassier, and there was plenty of random borrowing going on about the Complex, but then, getting to see and know something of his personality and lack of generosity, and realising how quick he was to tell some to bugger off, she had dismissed this thought as well. When no interest is at play and only a vacant concern applies, some things have to hit you in the face, she supposed.

She had finally figured it out sometime back, when she heard him knock on the door of the new neighbours next to her, (one of the myriad of new neighbours who had come and gone from the next door unit). He began by asking the young woman who answered the door, if he could speak to her man. When she said he was out, undeterred by this, he went on to introduce himself. Pointing in the direction of his own unit, he quite unashamedly and brashly, his confidence being what it was and unconcerned with being overheard, told her he could supply and if they ever had any requirements, they were welcome to come and see him. He told her he would do grass in small lots and up to as high an amount as they wanted to go. He was flexible and the quantity did not concern him. It was all business, after all. He had said, smiling and proudly.

The woman asked him a few diverting questions about the Complex itself and how long he had been there, thanked him suspiciously, said she would pass it onto her man and closed the door promptly, leaving him standing there alone for a moment. Aware that he had been dismissed, he gathered himself up, shrugged it off, and went on to his next venture.

It had answered many questions for her, like, why would anyone who earned such good money fibre-glassing want to live in this derelict and falling down, over-priced place (?). The answer was easy access to a large and reliable, constantly moving market.

It also gave a hint to him standing in front of her unit, speaking to Buff, on the first day of her arrival, and why he had been checking her door out over his shoulder at the time. He had clearly decided against his habitual first introduction of himself to newcomers, either deciding she was straight, or preferring to do so when there was a man about to talk business with. She knew he had no real love of women and he considered them an extension of the man they were with.

If they were on their own, then this was a foreign concept to him and it was something he could not understand, labelling them women who did not know their place in the scheme of things, and as such, should be ignored, and certainly never encouraged by doing any business direct with them. So, he simply never spoke to them. In fact, they were invisible to him, his gaze never locking onto any of them, even when he could not avoid a conversation for whatever reason, his eyes always hovering somewhere above their head.

There was no end of arse to this pillar of the community, with his long standing volunteer efforts for the Coastal group.

And, because of these voluntary labours, his continued popularity with the Town locals was assured, and just the way he liked it.

Arse, like the time when the rowdy young group who were his current next door neighbours, after twigging to what he was about, had, on a quiet night when he was out tried to break into his unit, after somehow, bypassing his Energetic Protection. Not getting very far though and only being successful in putting long cracks in the thick toughened glass of the sliding front door, no matter how relentless their joint efforts were. These doors were made to hold.

When seeing this ineffective attempt to enter his home, he just knew it had to be the group of youngsters who were now next door and him. Taking no crap from anyone, certainly not a bunch of kids, he called the Police. But only after transferring anything that might be of interest to them, to a trusted friends' home first. Doing a final check over the little unit for any forgotten apparatus before they arrived to do his bidding.

By the time the Police knocked on his door, it was obvious that this group had already vacated the Complex and gone their own merry way. Their sudden absence, probably what had alerted Davano to their probable guilt in the first place. Such coincidences too far a stretch for him to accept, so it had to be them, he was determined about that.

The Police spent all morning going over the place. They dusted for finger prints and they talked to those closest neighbours for any possibly worthwhile Statements, but none knew anything and all of them had heard zilch, their uninterested attitude impossible to get past for the local Constabulary. Much to the ire of Davano with his 'where is your bloody loyalty folks' and 'I will remember this later' glares, directed at all those concerned in the questioning. Not noticing their obvious annoyance over his expectations that they be drawn into any conversations with the Police on his behalf, either.

After doing all the usual things, finally, the Police prepared to leave, with a loudly vocal Davano saying, "Is that it? Aren't you even going to look for them?"

The Policemen telling him, "Yes, they would look, but really, what harm had been done? It was an assumption they had been trying to get in. Maybe they had just targeted him and only intended breaking the glass and causing a bit of mischief. After all, what did he have of value there really, that would prompt an actual break-in from neighbours who knew him, had been guests in his unit, and who would know the value of the belongings and contents there?" They had said this in a placating way but their questions had hung in the air. The Officers watched him with knowing looks.

After realising he had pushed his luck as far as it was going to go, Davano conceded that it was probably nothing really then, and he quietly let them go on their way, taking note of the whispered comments and wry looks they threw towards him as they got back into their Patrol car.

He had made sure anyway, that it had been a loud warning, and it would let everyone within hearing distance know to 'let that be a lesson to anyone else thinking of breaking into my place!' and he continued with his angrily thumping things about clean-up, muttering and swearing, just to add emphasise to his 'I meant it!' attitude, for those still bothering to watch his antics.

It amused her at the time, how Mr and Mrs Koin were nowhere to be seen out and about, while the Police sorted out this trouble with their favourite long term and well-paying tenant, who would pay to have the damages fixed anyway. They knew this was a surety. Their absence, a testament to their favouritism and their faith in him to handle such a minor thing without their assistance.

Just the same as it was okay, to have all these people coming and going from his unit but had been known to question others quickly, if the very same behaviour had taken place in their realm. After all, these things always depended on individual circumstances and had to be allotted individual treatment. Rules were made to be broken.

But now, she watched as the two men, talking quietly with each other, intent on whatever they were discussing, their heads bowed together, continued their walk toward the side entrance. Pleased that Buffs' usual gruff manner was current and not holding them up with any unnecessary and politically motivated conversation.

Funny, how the appearance of respectability, a well-paying and somewhat elitist profession and a load of well-known volunteer work (an editorial feature of the man himself in the main local News Paper helping things along) with an unusual and important to the whole Coast, group of volunteers, will do so much to encourage others to overlook the rumours or ignore the superior attitudes of any of their members. A downright, "No! Not our Davano" by others, was often said. She had even heard the comment of, "It's only jealousy!" from a few really solid supporters, the ones who had been nurtured specifically for this purpose. The fairy-tale, complete.

It was no real surprise, as these tactics had been long discovered by more serious people over the centuries, than this little big man. But, like so many others have found before him, that sometimes when nothing else can pull them up, something else seems to step in and give them the reckoning of their lifetime.

She didn't notice she had not seen Davano around for a while, since he was never one she concerned herself with at all. Something they shared in common, a mutual and unspoken agreement between them. Not thinking of it until she turned a corner onto the main road one day and almost bowled right into him coming the other way. This near collision had left them both unable to ignore each other, so putting her best foot forward, she chose politeness as her shield.

"Gosh Davano, I'm sorry, are you okay?" she asked, putting her hand out to steady him.

"Yes, no harm done," he replied, unable to ignore her now, looking down towards her, with his great height towering over her.

"Are you on holidays?" she had asked him, this being a week day and him not usually about then. She continued with her half-hearted polite strategy. Not really interested in why he was about during the working week but powerless to show this, consciously deciding ten minutes was the most she would give this interlude to their mutually agreed disdain for each other.

"No, I'm on Sick Leave and on strict instructions to take a passive walk around a few blocks a day, for daily exercise," he said.

And, as was his usual way, he looked over her head, never quite looking straight at her when he spoke to her. She had gotten over how disconcerting it was, trying to follow his roaming eyes. At another time she might have found a way to play with this, just to make a point and him uncomfortable, but not today.

Not sure how impolite it was to ask too much but knowing she had to show some concern, she asked hesitantly, "Why, what's wrong with you?"

"I've had a Heart Bypass," he declared, his tone admonishing as if she should have known this.

Instantly she thought of the hard drinking, hard smoking, party animal she had become familiar with, and wondered at how this was going to be a tough one for him to bear, let alone maintain.

"Your joking! When did this happen?" she asked, surprised and staggered, fumbling for something to say that would sound real. She stuck with the polite, time honoured responses. The ten minutes was ticking over, after all.

She noticed finally, the gaunt, sad look about his face. The blonde hair still at shoulder length, more limp and hanging in clumped dry tatters instead of the brushed and shiny gold it once was. How unkempt a character he now presented, as if he did not care anymore. She almost felt sorry for him.

Looking down at his feet, he replied, "On the way to work one morning, started on the bus and luckily, I got to work before I collapsed. Almost didn't make it!"

She shook her head slowly, truly amazed at this news. This was a man barely in his early forties, fit and strong, and yes, a wild life but... it only goes to show.

"I'm really sorry to hear it Davano, I had no idea. No one has mentioned it to me. Must be hard for you after being so active, hey?" she said cautiously, not wanting to stray too far onto provocative ground but unable to resist the small dig at him.

He gave a slight nod, "It's getting harder now that I'm on the improve. I watch a lot of videos, read, that sort of thing," he replied, a little more wistfully than he might have intended her to see.

She nodded at him, "What will you do, can you go back to your line of work?"

He smiled thoughtfully, looking out into the distance, to a time now seemingly in the distant past.

"No, I don't think so. I don't know yet what I will do or what I will be allowed to do. Taking one day at a time at the moment, just trying to survive this." His smile becoming a slight grimace in his efforts to maintain it, his face frozen and not quite working as he wanted it to.

She put a light hand on his arm, "Well, I'll let you go, won't keep you standing here needlessly, but you let me know if I can do anything to help you, won't you?"

She tried not to sound too enthusiastic, wanting to make sure he understood that she was only being polite, really. Reticent also, to offer any warmth to someone who had practised such callous and derogatory disregard for the female gender, all of his adult life. His eyes still roaming about now, with those old habits dying hard, if ever.

"Thanks, but Dan and his wife have been cooking for me. I'll be alright," he said, turning to watch her already walking away, figure. The look on his face as he watched her go, showing doubt in the sincerity of the offer she had just made. Job well done, that message clear, she had thought, satisfied at having achieved her goal.

"So! Hmmm!" She realised, as she had picked up her pace, watching the footpath passing beneath her feet as she went, it is a far cry from the money that comes in from fibre-glassing to the limited boundaries of a Disability Pension, with the allowable restrictions on earning money, and all the continued demands that go along with the permanent payment of it.

And, no more boozing. No more smoking. No more drugs. No more party animal. Then, she thought, no more ordering people around, no more standing over the little ones. She smiled, and glancing heavenwards she murmured, "Tough buggers!" She smiled at this, too.

Wondering if there would come a time when he would regret not trying out that luxury accommodation while he could afford it, because now, on a Pension, this place was as good as it was going to get if he wanted to remain living in this very expensive, party-hardy Resort Town.

She had also wondered at the level of support he was going to receive from the Koins now that he was no longer an earner of a good wage, or the holder of a prestige position. Somehow, she thought she already knew.

Now, she looked back at the two men heading toward the side entrance and the main road. Watched the smaller one kicking stones as he went, looking belligerent about whatever it was that had their rapt attention. Both, with heads bent, leaning together, and their quietly whispered conspiratorial tones, the animated nods and shakes that went with them. She watched until they turned onto the footpath and disappeared around the corner.

She never saw Davano up close again, only spotting him off in the distance, head down, and his neglected appearance seeming foreign and strange on the once confident man.

Her questions were answered though, to the level of support he would now receive, and not only from the Koins. She had watched, as those who reacted like a hunting predator having spotted wounded prey close by, took great enjoyment in their teasing sport but kept their sights honed on the Game that was about. And, their unspoken delight in long awaited revenge was drawn out and relentless.

SIMON

The screams grew, then, receded again. The thumping sounds of running and jumping feet hitting wooden floorboards growing louder in the quiet of the night, then stillness.

Noise again.

This had been going on for some time now but since it came from the direction of Simons' two storey unit block, no one was taking much notice. Except now, with the lateness of the hour, it was becoming annoying to those whose work the following day required some sleep, at least.

Simon's dalliance with Call Girls was a well-known occurrence, and also well-known, was that these dalliances tended to take place when he was on a bender with his well-loved Speed. They would play some favoured game of Simons' such as Hide-n-seek and Chase or Catch as Can, and were always a prelude to whatever else went on. Neighbours close-by would sigh and shake their heads but say little else about the latest bout that was in progress, their past complaints always welcomed with a self-satisfied grin from Simon.

He was a young man of thirty something, but given his physical condition it was hard to be sure. He had lived here at

Koins for eight years or more, and he had the all too common attitude that this gave him some sort of priority over other tenants. An attitude that bothered no one and was shown to only a few, with him keeping to himself generally, and his frequent, dedicated periods of compulsive self-imposed hibernation saved anyone from really feeling the effects of this supposed priority. Indeed, there were those who had never laid eyes on him, only discovering his existence from their first frightening experience with his periodic game playing.

So, for the most part, no one ever saw him out and about. Him, choosing the hidden, closed off dark confines of his unit, door locked against the outside world and watching his perpetually going videos, completely in the grasp of his Speed addiction.

He had an ex-wife and child somewhere, from the days when he had lived a reasonably normal life, but he never saw them anymore. Had, in fact, no idea where they even were. He had made a conscious decision some years ago to hibernate with his needle, and he saw no reason to even try for anything else now. Content with the world he had created and unable to find the stamina and determination needed for any major changes, the endeavour too great to consider, he accepted himself as he was.

She had first met Simon when asked by Mrs Koin if she could deliver an envelope to him on her way down to her own unit. Such little requests were commonplace and often. Most of those approached, realised that to say yes to the smaller requests gave them opportunity to go unnoticed when saying no to the larger, more unwelcome ones. All of these small strategies were tools in the Self-Survival pack, and learned quickly by the majority. Simon had opened the door a crack, peeking out at her. He had swung the door wide with a grin on his face when seeing there was a female waiting at his door.

"Hello," she said hesitantly, keeping her hand on the outside door frame she had been leaning on.

"Delivery from Mrs Koin for you," she had followed almost amicably, waving the envelope at him, put off by the eerily dark interior and the great bulk of the man standing there, naked to his enormous waist, wearing only dirty crumpled shorts with splattering's of ancient food dotted all over them, bits and pieces here and there, still solid and hanging. The smell that met her was dull and dead, like the air that might come from a sealed up tomb.

He reached out and grabbing her arm, steering her inside as he said, "Hi, come in, come in, darlin!" His black toothed grin spread broad for her.

Momentarily unsure, she glanced around taking in the unbelievable state of the place, deciding in an instant she was not going too far from the front door, her confidence slipping.

He maintained his hold on her arm, his eyes watching the spot where he slowly and imperceptibly rubbed his finger against her skin, enjoying the feel of her soft flesh.

She shivered but did not pull away.

The ripped and tattered curtains, drawn against the light of day, only small cracks showing light here and there, were a permanent barrier and a protector from the world outside. The dust floating in the air glimmered in the rare pools of light, as every movement they made caused small eddies to take to the air. Things were strewn all about the cluttered floor and piled high on any available spaces on the high bookshelves, which lined the four walls. Empty dirty dinner plates covered most of the small coffee table, only a corner left for other uses and now inhabited by an old chipped bowl full of the paraphernalia needed for drug use. He made no effort to move it or hide it away from her. Her eyes settled on the small bowl. With no embarrassment, he ignored her perusal. His attention was for her alone. He kept his light grip on her arm.

Within reaching distance to the coffee table, sat one enormous and prehistoric armchair. Facing the ancient armchair, and on the other side of the coffee table, was the biggest flat screen television she had ever seen. A lone monument to luxury, it took up a goodly section of the wall on that side of the room, and was pressed comfortably between the book shelves, high up on the wall, there.

The putrid smell of the place taking a hold on her as she went deeper into this black void, and was most appalling to her senses. She glanced toward the filthy kitchen, aware that she might be sick at any moment now. She made an effort to control her disagreeing stomach. Mindful, she would not last much longer.

Trying to keep her focus on the young man opposite her, she saw how greyness tinged the pallid white skin which hung on his over-weight frame. The wide grin showing a mouthful of blackened, chipped and broken stubs of teeth, and the rotting smell that came with every outward breath he took only added to the nausea she felt, testing her ability at control, even more. He was a tall, round, vast splotch of jellied flesh in the centre of the room. Standing there, with only his pair of loose fitting, filthy shorts on.

She did not know whether to be frightened or sad for him at first, but after the initial scare subsided a little, she could not help but feel pity for this lonely, wasted and still young person.

Trying to settle her moving stomach and needing to get further away from the rotting smell coming from his mouth, with a little effort she moved her arm away from under his hand and his roaming fingers, distracting him with light conversation as she did so. Taking this opportunity to move a few steps back from him, she had stood chatting with him for only a while. He was happy to tell her his life story so long as she was happy to stand there and listen to him. With a tirade a words tumbling over each other so quickly, then every so often, he would wander off, his focus shifting elsewhere with his memories, his eyes glazed and vacant. Helped by his drugged state, his speech slipping into a mumbled incoherent buzz, and then he would rouse himself again just as quickly, and continue on as if the distraction had never happened. She had said her farewells as soon as she felt she could and left the young man to close the door once again, on the outside world he no longer felt a part of.

The screaming and cut off laughter, rising in the still night air again.

Someone yelled out, "Fuck you Simon! SHUT-UP!!!!"

The thumping stopped abruptly, the perpetrator momentarily pausing, listening to the yelled request. Someone called back, "Ahh, you shut up, yourself!"

Silence again.

Most, who knew Simon gave him leeway out of sympathy. Others, who were passing through and never saw him let alone met him, would complain the next day to Mr and Mrs Koin but apart from their scowls in his direction, they generally left him alone, too. The familiarity of eight years of tenancy dampening the impact of any misbehaviour or small misdemeanours.

Once, he had come to see her, his thong'ed feet slapping the ground as he walked, his large bulk bouncing along. His head perched on his shoulders, looking as if blown out of his body in the same way the nipple is pushed out of an inflating balloon, to cry on her shoulder about his overspending of his Disability Pension and him getting behind in his rent, and, "What will I do!!?" But then, following it up in his habitually abrupt way, with, "Mrs Koin will give me time," he had gone as unexpectedly as he came. Leaving her wondering and curious, about his real motives for this rare visit. Finally, she settled on the truth of his loneliness, and the unwelcome status he carried with the other tenants, leaving her to be the only choice he had really had.

On this night, they had known a fairly substantial storm was moving in over the Coast. While everyone took notice of the Storm Warnings sounding on the Radio and Television Stations, it was a common enough and expected occurrence at this time of the year for the tropical Coast, so no one was prone to any panic. Quietly going about the business of making sure nothing was lying loosely around the yards and tying down the things that could be fastened, being sure not to overlook even the most innocent of possible projectiles. Getting rid of hanging branches, and digging out any of the already blocked drains which helped to carry the extra load of water that was bound to travel along them soon.

The Supermarkets filled with calm and mostly silent people, buying extra food and stocking up on bottled water, the shelves slowly and predictably emptying.

Everyone was doing their bit in their own environment, and the ground crews could already be seen, in tight little groups around the town, checking off their list of things to take care of. The annual experience of dealing with the seasonal storms and the lessons already learnt from the past, showing in their methodically expert way of going about their work.

By nightfall the storm was in full flight. The wind was rattling and shaking the windows in fury, sounding more and more like an angry invader wanting to come in. The rain, pelting down in one continued flow, was thunderous on the rooves, making it impossible to hear the televisions or radios no matter how loud the volume switch was turned up. The wind whistled shrilly through the cracks in the walls, only adding to cacophony surrounding her. Lightening flashed and crackled overhead, and counting the seconds between the flashes and the bangs the thunder made, was a pastime practised by many, and used as a slight distraction to the frightening and impressive display being put on by Mother Nature.

There would be trees downed tomorrow. Those, which had become too top heavy for the soft, water logged soil to hold onto, would have paid the price for their untenable and exposed positions. She spared a thought for the Emergency workers who were bound to be out and about already in this horrible weather, and for all the Emergency volunteers who would be busy in the days to come, helping to patch up and cover all the roofs out there, that had been breached by the ferocious winds and pounding rain.

The flash flooding was a given with these type of storms. The huge amount of water dumped so quickly, making it impossible for the drains to cope. Even the massive stormwater drains would fall, the great deluge coming at them making them seem impotent and tiny.

She dug in for the night, deciding a good book and bed was the best way to go. Hoping the flooding would not involve them or the Complex, and hoping that the dilapidated, crumbling buildings they all called home for the moment, would stand up to the uncontrollable force raging outside. She would keep her fingers crossed. Just in case.

The next morning, the rising sun and fresh sweet air denied the wildness of the night before. Only the mess left by the efficient destruction, and strewn all over the ground everywhere, telling the truth of the event. Broken branches and leaves were all over the roadways. The bedlam, spread all over the streets and making for slow pickings by the cars trying to travel along them, mixed with the dirt washed from garden beds and yards and leaving days of clean up time ahead, were dangerous for pedestrians and motorists, alike.

Her television had gone to snow and now, on this lovely fresh aired morning, standing outside looking up at the communal aerial on the roof, she saw that it had fallen over sideways, another victim of the high wind from the previous night. She looked around, aware that everyone who was using this connection must be having the same trouble. So, where were they?

All was silent as a graveyard. The broken branches and debris still lying where it fell, the tenants uninterested in coming out to inspect the damage yet, preferring to prolong the eventual clean-up that would be needed by them, if they were to navigate their comings and goings with a clear passage again, anytime soon.

A young fellow on his way to his car came out of his unit and glanced in her direction, nodding his head in polite greeting, as he opened his car door.

"Are you having trouble with your television?" she called to him.

"No, I use an indoor antenna," he replied, deserting the open car door and walking slowly towards her, his curiosity apparent.

"The aerial has blown over. You're a young bloke, can you go up there and fix it?" she asked him hopefully.

He looked toward the roof, "No, you've got to be kidding!!" he answered, disbelieving of her request and shaking his head. "That is an asbestos roof, I'm not going up there!" he finished.

She glanced at the roofs on the rest of the buildings and saw that they too, were the same smoky grey stuff that hers was made of.

"You're sure?" she asked hesitantly, "Are all of them asbestos?"

The young man nodded at her.

Well, that explained why the Complex had been left to go to rack and ruin over all of these years. Too much money to get rid of the huge amount of asbestos, which was covering every building in the Complex and probably all of the internal walls, too. As was Law, if you started to work on anything with asbestos in it, you had to call in the Specialists to remove it all first. They would come, covered head to toe in their white plastic coveralls, and then submit a Bill of extraordinary costs at the end of it all.

"Just use an indoor antenna," he advised, walking back in the direction of his parked car. His offered solution, an easier way to solve the complicated problem that he wanted no part of. Just ignore it and work around it, was the convenient foundation the whole place now seemed to operate on.

"Okay," she murmured, still looking at the roof and realising how uncomfortable she felt about living beneath it.

She hoped there would come a day, when the Law would extend to protecting the uninformed and change the status of allowing human habitation in such places, too. Changing such a status would force people to take the responsibility on, for their own shit pile. She did not like feeling like an expendable and unprotected component, to someone else's convenience. She never could get used to how cheap, and usable, human life was to some.

She was still standing there, taking a good look around at all the asbestos roofing and wondering at the incredible cost it would be to remove it, the young fellow had already driven off in his car, when, glancing around at the sound of an odd scraping noise, she saw a near naked girl at Simmons' place. After opening a ground floor window and carefully lifting a chair through it to the ground, she was covertly and cautiously, climbing backwards, feet first, bum in the air, out of it. Dangling there for a moment, her feet looking for purchase on the chair and then dropping the rest of the way, the chair tipping sideways then righting itself, as her weight hit it.

"Oh! What now!" She said, as she started towards the girl, who, having seen her, lifted a finger to her lips telling her to, "Shush!"

From a distance, she was looking at a little round dwarf. The full figure made to look even more voluptuous, by the shortness of the girl. Wearing a pair of skimpy panties and a man's shirt, held together by one button only, emphasizing her large bobbing and swaying breasts. Her lovely long wavy brunette hair in a wild halo around her head, framed a very beautiful heart shaped and extremely young looking face.

While she was walking slowly toward the girl, she was dashing barefoot in a strange looking kind of a dance, half on tip toes to protect against the prickles growing all over the ground, towards her.

Frightened, she whispered, "Please, be quiet, I think he has passed out."

She looked at the girls' dirty, unclad feet and said, "Who are you, what's going on?"

The girl, struggling to get her breath and taking deep gulps, still in a panic, stuttered in reply, "He locked me in the bedroom. I have been trying to escape for a few days now!" "I think I broke the window," she added absentmindedly, her shock making this insignificant thing seem more important than it could be, given that she had been a hostage of some kind. She was twisting her hands together, drops of blood showing from the small cuts all over them.

The girl was clearly distressed, and the shock was setting in fast with her newfound freedom. The twisting hands continued, round and round, as her hands grew a deep red, and not just from the dripping and spreading blood. She put an arm around her and started walking her toward the safety of her own unit.

"Come with me. I have you, all is well now, you are safe," she told her confidently, looking to sooth her more than anything else, because she knew there was no way Simon was going to interfere with this rescue, not over her live body, anyway.

It turned out the young girl was a Call Girl who had taken Simons' fancy. So much so, he had slipped her a 'knock-out' pill of some kind from his substantial stash, and locked her away in one of the spare bedrooms. Her mind boggled at the vision of this tiny, beautiful creature and the huge, jellied blob that was Simon. She would not have stood a chance if he had ever become really serious in his intent.

He had not tied her up or anything truly nasty like that, he had simply locked her away and refused to let her go. In his strange fantasy world, the girl was captured and imprisoned for him to look at, like a beautiful butterfly. She remembered his fascination over the feel of her skin, and his roaming finger on her arm. She shivered again at the thought.

"Why didn't you call out? Someone would have heard you, there are people everywhere here!" she had asked the distraught girl.

"I did, I did!" she answered in a whining and wobbly voice, "For two days now, and no one took any notice," she stammered, glancing around the Complex, her look condemning and disbelieving.

"I thought I would never get away. I thought, I thought...," she began to cry again, her hands still twisting were beginning to go a very maroon, blood red colour.

"I was so frightened, I thought I was a gonna!" she finally got out, the tears began to roll down her lovely heart shaped face.

"He's a bloody nutter!" she gasped, looking for her anger. "A bloody weirdo!" In her shock, and as if to steady herself, she had to repeat this over and over, in little more than a whisper, relieving some of the distress that was threatening to overwhelm her.

That is what happens when all that screaming and game playing is just the norm. She told the girl of this, trying to settle her and to offer some sort of excuse for those around them, who had ignored her pleas' for their intervention. Undoubtedly, people had heard her and simply dismissed it as none of their business, going about their own busy routines.

There is something to be said for the desensitizing of the in-house population, with all the odd kinds of conflicts and the weird habits of others that they all live with here daily, she had told the girl.

They are not really to blame completely, for their inability to have found her and rescued her sooner.

"Come on then, this time we call the Police, let them take care of it," she told her, still holding on firmly to her, frightened that if she let go, the young woman might just collapse to the ground, she was shaking so much all over.

"I won't get into trouble, will I?" Her young face looking even more worried than it already was, for the illegality of her Profession. The tears leaving clean tracks amid the grime on her lovely face, her huge amber eyes bigger than ever.

"We'll see, okay? Doesn't matter, anyway. It has to be done," suspecting that kidnapping and imprisonment might take priority over prostitution, she had thought with some amusement, and she had taken the girl inside to wait for their arrival.

Later, thinking maybe, she should have just dumped it all in Mr and Mrs Koins' lap. She knew how adept they could be, in turning something serious into nothing, and vice versa. It might do some good for them to see how severe things could really get around here. But she quickly realised, no, the girl did not deserve that, not after what she had already been through.

This was one she would happily leave for the Police to tell them of, although, slightly wishing she could be a fly on the wall at the time, when they did tell them. A spiteful thought, and one that she enjoyed immensely.

She could already see the look of innocence on Mrs Koins' face, as she manages to forget all the previous complaints about their noisy, game playing tenant. Her prescience, conveniently forgotten.

As she says, "There must be some misunderstanding, Simon would not do such a thing!"

And, as she resolutely sides with her well-paying and long standing tenant before she finally, and fittingly, yields saying, "We'll pray for him this Sunday!"

WARWICK

"G'day babe!"

She swung around to look behind her at the sound of the, not quite pronounced right, greeting, called to her from down the far end of the main driveway, already sure she knew who it was.

Warwick had a way of not quite saying his words with a beginning to, or an end to them. Almost as if he could not get his tongue to twist the right way to make the needed sounds, sometimes making it difficult to understand him, and generally earning from strangers unused to this, the declaration that he was drunk, or otherwise influenced by some sort of drug. It was not a conclusion that went too far from the mark, either.

Warwick was a seriously committed follower of anything containing alcohol. But, he was also a hard worker, who would take on any job for a time that would bring in good money, and he had not turned down stints at oyster shucking, which had you standing on concrete floors from five a.m. in the morning for very long twelve hour shifts and was not for the faint-hearted, to any menial cleaning job fill-ins, if needs' be, to keep him employed and the money coming in. So, he was popular and more often than not, tolerated.

He had worked alongside her in the strawberry fields, and while they had rarely spoken more than a greeting in those days, the connection seemed to offer him solace and he always greeted her warmly on the rare occasions they saw each other nowadays.

A bit of a contradiction in so many ways, you could never really feel like you knew him. He was also one of the most fabulous looking young men you would be likely to ever see. He was fit and toned, with rippling muscles that looked like he worked out in a gym for hours every day. A perfectly small waist and great solid calf muscles, all covered by the most beautiful tan from his pretty blond head to his toes. Looking like some Greek Adonis, no doors were closed to him, and every job he applied for, he got. Whether it needed strength to move and pack great bags of horse feed or pushing a light little mop around an office block, he got them all.

She had always wondered why, the one most obvious job of Modelling, which such God-given natural beauty would synch, was the one he had never tried for, or even thought of.

She remembered a night of celebration at the local RSL Club, in honour of a strawberry season completed for another back-breaking year. How, he had taken over the dance floor all night. Refusing to leave his glass of ale on any of the nearby tables, and managing to throw himself around wildly while maintaining a firm grip on his drink, but splashing protesting dancers all around him. Laughingly ignoring the bouncers chasing him around the dance floor and their efforts to passively get their messages through to him, on the other hand, generously paying for the taxis' home for everyone in their little group that night.

The only thing lacking for Warwick though, was the one thing you had to have for success in life and to round out and complete that fabulous physical frame. You needed a functioning personality or maybe, a little unkindly, you needed a brain that was capable of some kind of rational thought.

Talk about, the lights are on but nobody is home.

It seemed like some cruel joke by Mother Nature, to have given such natural offerings but not to have completed the package at the final moment. You know, a last minute wave of a hurried hand, with a, 'There, you'll do!' by a rushing Mother Nature who had a train to catch as it was leaving the station.

To a degree, he seemed unaware of his physical attributes, but then, he seemed very aware of them. Coming to life when a female, any female, came into his surroundings. When he would instantly, turn into this quiet and brooding sexy Movie Star type, softly murmuring his characteristically slurred sounds while looming closely over them. Bringing, unnoticed by him, grins to everyone else's faces who might have been watching on.

Then, there were the times, he had come to stand in front of someone with the accusation he had seen them up the street, ducking into a shop just because they had wanted to avoid him when they saw him coming the other way, and declaring, "Why does everyone do that to me?" With an, "I hate that! Why do that?" sounding like a sullen child, and often leaving an innocent and bewildered person in his stead, as he rushed off again.

She turned around to wait up for him approaching her with hasty steps. He looked well-groomed and neat and stylish, in his pressed slacks and casual shirt. His boots gleamed in the sunlight.

"Hello, haven't seen you for a while," she called to him as he came closer, glad to see the smile on his face suggested good tidings, this time.

"Guess what!" he said as he reached her, impatiently launching straight in with his news, "I'm moving!" he gushed.

"Well, that can only be a good thing," she replied as she glanced about wryly, adding with as much interest as she could muster for this unpredictable and overgrown kid, "Tell me all about it."

She often felt like she was talking to a small child whenever she spoke with Warwick. Always having to watch how you said something, and making sure to keep it to basic words. He tended to think you were having a go at him when you threw words at him that he could not understand, and his reactions would be swift and sure, turning any casual encounter into an unnecessary confrontation. He had a short fuse you did not want to light.

"I've met a lady, and I'm moving in with her!" he said, the big smile all over his face.

Choosing her words carefully now, and not just because of his past volatility but because she did not want to put a damper on his newfound joy, and the excitement it gave him. Still hugging him, she asked, "Is it something that is secure for you? What happens if it does not work out?" walking a fine line, trying hard not to sound too negative.

Releasing his grip on her, he smiled again at her, "That won't happen, she's an older lady, she owns the house, and she just loves me!" he said, emphasizing the last.

She frowned, unsure how any of that answered her question, but she decided it was as far as her comments would go, knowing better than to embark on any lectures to him. Besides, maybe this is just what this man/child needed. Maybe a rich older woman, who loved his brawn and was grateful for no brain, would look after him in the kind of luxury and tender consideration he had never known in his young life before. In some way, the hardworking, female loving Warwick deserved this kind of outcome. Horses for courses, she supposed, and this fellow was born for this type of role.

Diplomatically, she went on, "No more drunken outbursts then, she won't be able to handle that!" She continued quickly, "She will be gone, and you will have lost your chance," still trying for a conversational tone to her words of warning.

He replied, "Oh, I know! I have been landscaping her garden too!" as if this offered some kind of proof of his faithful journey on the straight and narrow, his grin growing impossibly broader.

Knowing she was never going to get anywhere with mere words, shaking her head and giving up on him, she gave him another warm hug and wished him well, but she had her doubts.

His affair with alcohol had been the most important one in his life so far, and she remembered the day he nearly took everyone out, in his drunken state, who had tried to stop him from demolishing his bathroom with an enormous sledge hammer.

It was on one of the occasions Mr and Mrs Koins' daughter was visiting, down from the farm for a few days stay. And, as was her habit at those times, she had been checking over the Complex and its' tenants and generally being the enthusiastic and supportive daughter, while her 'in your face' presence reminded everyone that she had the last and final say, in the end. She had this display of hers honed to perfection, and most tenants, those who did not duck for cover quickly enough, were completely bluffed by her and exceptionally polite, almost reverent, as she passed by them.

It was not a good time to poke your head up, let alone put on a display of drunken violent frustration, at the non-functioning toilet and overworked plumbing in your overpriced unit, but that is exactly what Warwick did.

Warwick shared the top floor above Simon with a reasonable young man, who generally, could keep him in some semblance of control. But, on this Saturday morning, the young man was out and about with his new girlfriend, leaving Warwick to his own weekend delights. The banging noises here and there, had begun around lunchtime, but when they became louder and more frequent, broken by loud curses and profanities, the sounds of walls splintering and tiles cracking loudly, Simon had come outside to yell up the external stairs. Another one of those, do as I say, not do as I do, occasions.

"Put a fucking lid on all the bloody noise, will you Warwick!"

Warwick stuck his head out the door and screamed, "You… FUCK OFF!" waving the great hammer he had clasped firmly in one hand, at Simon.

The banging began again.

"Some nerve, Simon. Look who is talking!" someone close by yelled back at Simon.

The curses, louder now, as an unsure Simon, glancing around and deciding he did not really want to buy into this one, including the nearby unknown commentator, and choosing the prudent path, saying nothing more, went back into his own unit and quietly closed the door, disappearing into his cool, dark world as if he had never tried to intervene.

It only took another half an hour of all this noisy annihilation, before Mr and Mrs Koins' daughter appeared in the doorway of the little Office.

"What the hell is he DOING!?" she demanded loudly from no one in particular. "What is the dammed idiot up to, now?" she muttered, as she marched up the outside stairs, to stand in Warwick's open doorway.

"What the bloody hell is going on in here?" she yelled confidently, down the hallway.

An angry, dishevelled and very drunk Warwick came out of his bathroom and stormed towards her, one raised arm and still holding the huge hammer, screaming defiantly, "And you… FUCK OFF TOO!" He slammed the front door closed in her face.

"Jesus!" she said shakily, as she started back down the creaking stairway, on her way to look for supportive reinforcements. The numerous bands of gold on her fingers clacking on the metal of the old paint bare handrail as she went, the sounds keeping time with every step downwards she took. It was another half an hour before the Police car pulled into the main driveway, coming to a stop by the small group standing talking amongst themselves, in front of the open Office doors.

A bathroom wash basin, a toilet seat, half a cistern and associated unidentifiable bits and pieces had been hauled out of the small bathroom window, along with lots of growing curses, in the time it had taken for them to arrive at the Complex. The small group waiting helplessly, simply watched on.

The pile on the ground under the high window surely growing, with the strenuous and continued efforts of the man still leaning out of it, who now, seeing the two Officers getting out of the Patrol car parked in the driveway, waving a hammer filled hand at them, screamed, "And you, you fuckers, why don't you do something about these CUNTS!?" pointing with his hammer at the whole group in general. Naked to the waist, sweat glistened and ran over his bronzed skin, dripping onto his shoulders from his wet golden hair.

"You don't care if they steal from us, hey?" spit spraying the air, his tongue tripping over the words. "That's okay, isn't it? Who cares about us, hey? Not you arseholes, suck arses all of you!"

The words sounding slightly hilarious with their not quite said right inflections, was made so much worse by drunkenness. Giving all those pretending not to be home but who were watching behind their closed doors, enthralled and determined to bear witness to Warwicks' supposed and imminent demise, reason to smile and much to laugh about later.

The two Officers slowly walked up the outside stairs, speaking quietly, trying to calm Warwick as they came, hopeful still, in their quest to restore sanity to the drunken and violent man before random damage became real harm to someone, "Come on mate," and, "that's enough now, open the door!"

The one following his partner up the stairs was taking a furtive good look around at the general layout, not liking the restrictions of the high, narrow stairway.

"You have made your point now, time to give it up," the first Officer was saying, his tone softly persuasive and encouraging, "put the hammer down, open the door and you can tell me what's up, okay?" as if Warwick was a naughty child determined to have their way.

Surprisingly, Warwick opened the door as casually as if he was inviting old friends in.

The young Officers did not relax at this offering though, with one staying protectively behind his partner. With hand relaxing on his hip, negating the fact that he had his hand lightly resting over his gun and was not just adopting a nonchalant position to stand in at all, staying alert and rigid in their gentle approach.

There was ten minutes or so of chatter between them, with Warwick standing in the open doorway, they did not try to force their way in further. The first Officer, keeping his hand out in his request for Warwick to hand over the large hammer, then finally, after Warwick hanging his head and listening for a bit, gently put the hammer into the Officers open hand. Sober enough to realise his lost cause in the face of these two, whose job it was to resolve this situation and who would not walk away from it, no matter what he had to say about his unfair predicament. The Officer handed the hammer onto his Partner behind him, keeping himself free and clear to deal with the unpredictable, blubbering Warwick. The Koins, still watching from the bottom of the dated stairway, remained silent and unmoving, eyes wide, not wanting to cause any distraction or give reason for the upset man to lash out again, aware of how tenuous the moment was.

His submission taking them off guard for that instant and catching them unawares, and Warwick taking this opportunity, spun around and in four running steps, dashed to the second floor windows on the other side of the lounge room. Throwing one leg over the ledge, hanging onto each side of the window frame with his hands, he threatened to jump onto the concrete walkway below.

It was all very dramatic.

The two Police Officers were right behind him, only momentarily taken aback. Grabbing him, one wrapping an arm around his neck, the other throwing himself around Warwick's thickly muscled torso, they wrestled him awkwardly, back inside. The noise was deafening, and frightening for anyone downstairs waiting, unable to see what was going on. A bellowing Warwick and yelling Police Officers, but the rest of the Complex seemingly still, holding its' breath, suspended in time, even the birds seemed quieter.

Passing the Koins on his way to the Patrol car, in a moment of strange and sinister calm, Warwick whispered to them, "Still got you a beauty, now everyone knows about you bunch of thieves!"

They herded him, blubbering again and cuffed, into the back seat of the Police car, while the Koins went up to survey the extent of the mad destruction to the old bathroom.

The Koins would forgive him, as was their nature, so long as he paid for their brand new, upcoming bathroom and toilet ("That worked out well," they would say to each other, when inspecting the new work), and the rest of the tenants would comment to each other, when discussing it over a coffee or two, that they should have let the silly bugger jump.

VANESSA
AND THE BREAK-IN

Tall, thin and always a strange colour of whitish grey, giving away the many years addicted to injecting speed, Vanessa could often be found fishing off the pier, down along the Esplanade, with her young son, who, in her way, she was devoted to. The pair, happy and delighted over any catch they had, no matter how big or small the fish might be, and their obvious quality time spent together was enjoyed by anyone who watched their antics. He never went without anything, she saw to that, and he was a happy, precocious and thriving child who everyone liked to see coming and they gave freely of their time whenever he needed a helping hand with something that only a man could solve for him, like fixing his bicycle, or the like. It was at those times that Vanessa tolerated the contact with her neighbours, watching on from a distance.

They had lived upstairs next to Warwick's unit for over ten years, and she carried her air of confident entitlement openly whenever she had to have dealings with any of the other tenants, whom she generally ignored if she could, expressing genuine annoyance and lack of patience, when she could not. For the most part she kept to herself, only spending time with her many and varied outside friends and visitors. That is, until a much younger couple with a newborn baby, moved into the unit on the other side of her.

For some reason, which became harder and harder to fathom, Vanessa took an instant dislike to the new young woman and what had started out as glares and general rudeness towards her, spiralled into something loudly abusive and deeply offensive. Even the hardened neighbours who surrounded them were shocked. More than a few of them, provoked into feeling inclined to take on the usually unwanted role of observer, in the least, and umpire, when it became dire. All of this, making for a very unpopular Vanessa and dragging her into the limelight she usually liked to avoid.

The younger woman had made it a habit to come out daily with her broom and sweep the stairs. Spending time to sweep the concrete driveway below too, her new baby strapped to her. Seemingly, using the time to remind herself of the continued existence of the outside world and to take a break from the restriction of indoors, getting some fresh air and sun. She would potter about in her small garden and sit with her baby in the sunshine for a while, relieving the tedium of her confined world.

Vanessa begun to use these times to her full advantage, to stand in her doorway, at first scowling at the young woman with her baby, then mumbling towards her, and finally, when this appeared to have no effect, progressing to outright loud abuse.

"You're a rotten mother!" she would yell. "Get up and feed your baby, it's always crying!" she would scream, going a bright red in the face.

"What do you do with your time, you lazy bitch!" and she would throw her a look of pure hatred. The young mother, not wanting to feed her wrath and frightened by her ranting and her apparent serious intent, would go inside rather than respond to the malicious display. And the whole process would repeat itself again the very next day.

The rest of the Complex realised there was a real problem developing when Vanessa began coming outside of her unit and into the middle of the driveway, to yell abuse at the young neighbours every time the newborn cried. Seeing how newborns do this every time they need a feed, this started to become more than an annoyance for everyone, and not just the immediate neighbours who had to listen to her yelling, "Shut that kid up!" at all hours of the day and into the wee hours of night.

She seemed able and ready, with an instant response, the moment the little one gave so much as a peep. And, with it not mattering what time of the day or night it was, had a few accusing Vanessa of being downright selfish and self-centred. Some, telling her it was her that was keeping them all up and not the crying baby, so "Pull your bloody head in, before someone knocks it off for you!" she was told in no uncertain terms, the seriousness of those involved gearing up a notch or two.

It almost became creepy, this apparent lying in wait.

The young mother, growing more and more nervous and worried as the days went by, began seeking the protection of Mr and Mrs Koin, who at first, thought it would blow over and were yet to take any of it very seriously, fobbing it off with a wave of the hand. It was a small thing, compared to history.

Soon, everyone took their turn in asking Vanessa what her problem was, and more than one argument broke out when a belligerent Vanessa promptly told them to, "Bugger off and mind your own bloody business, you bunch of useless shits!"

The poor young woman, already under the natural stress of dealing with a newborn and the lost hours of sleep that comes with it, would only look at her, bleary eyed, when she saw her, as if she was some new and unidentified species, and would say nothing. Tiredness and fear, convincing her that the Koins' were probably right, and she would leave it to them to handle any concerns over the developing displays. It all came to a head when Mrs Koin, finally, stepped into the fray to champion the young mother.

Vanessa was issued with an official looking Warning and told to leave the young ones alone, if she wanted to continue her tenancy there. She was to respect her neighbours and their rights to a normal life, and that all the rubbish was to stop.

It was an enjoyment for all the other inhabitants with long memories, and caused much appreciative gossip and back-slapping about the entitled Vanessa getting her dues, and a 'How's that!' for any previously displayed importance over them.

"Time someone put her in her place!" a few of them commented. Sure to do so within earshot of the arrogant Vanessa, who would wave her clenched fist at them, cursing quietly and under her breath, with the warning to behave still ringing in her ears.

The yelling at the new neighbours did stop, much to the relief of the other tenants, but the filthy glares toward the young woman did not, and the seething Vanessa's annoyance at what she saw as a lack of loyalty from the Koins, toward someone who had been paying their rather large rents for ten years, just kept building.

Her usual dislike for the other neighbours now grew into outright anger, with her totally ignoring everyone who crossed her path, her nose pointed decidedly skywards, like a child embarrassed by a scolding from her parents. Anyone who gave it any real thought or had previous experiences with Vanessa, knew that this was only the beginning and far from over, and was only going to get worse. Like a dog with a good bone, Vanessa would never let go of a slight, she would hang on for dear life.

Finally, after the enthusiastic slap across Rita's face, the Koins issued Vanessa with a firm and final Eviction Notice.

Rita's favourite pastime had always been that of the Town Crier. Only the new residents would fall into the trap of offering any information about themselves in casual conversation, to an interested and inquisitive Rita. She had a remarkable ability to turn the smallest offering into something akin to a saga, and would make sure that anyone who made the mistake of speaking with her at all, would hear all about whatever she saw, was the latest juicy titbit. She was always unkind to the female tenants, and a stubbed toe turned into a broken foot every time. Truth and Rita, could never be accused of being good friends.

Most everyone would choose to just avoid Rita, but when Vanessa took the more direct approach, anyone who had been previously burnt, stood quietly by and cheered her on. There were those, torn between her madness toward the young mother and her baby, and their support for this latest stand. And it was with, almost, some sadness to them, that such a heroic action had ended up being the excuse for her eventual eviction.

It was a surprise to the other tenants anyway, to see this Final Eviction Notice, at all. Those, who had seen the likes of Alexander and Warwick's multitude of indiscretions forgiven, once all the costs had been paid by them of course, had trouble weighing the balance here. Not forgetting, Vanessa was not the only one who would be included in their forthcoming homeless, status. She had a little son too, and Koins Motel was pretty much, the only home he had known in his young life so far. After all, these tiffs between tenants were a fairly normal and common occurrence and they generally blew over with time running its' course. And, as always, people growing bored with whatever the cause had really been, as the original argument became old and worn out news.

Nobody said anything when Vanessa protested loudly to them that, "They want me out of the unit because they can get more for it, from a new tenant who wouldn't restrict their rent rises because of any current and standing Tenancy Agreement." And, "They are keeping the Bond, so they get that too! It's all too convenient for them!" Choosing the safe side, they only shrugged at her sadly.

Her announcements and complaints, directed at no one in particular, satisfying her need to spread a little mud around, and leaving her feeling a little less helpless. Even the softer, kind-hearted ones, listening with a sympathetic ear to her claims that they would both be, "On the streets and the Koins won't care!" could do nothing to placate her, her motor mouth locked into top gear.

When the day of the departure deadline arrived, she ran into a still fuming Vanessa, who was packing boxes into a friend's trailer parked in the driveway, so she stopped to wish her and her young son well on their way. Not feeling too sad for them really, she believed that Providence worked in strange ways and that these things generally worked out for the betterment of everyone involved, taking you onto new pastures and potential opportunities. That maybe, Vanessa had been here too long, stagnating. And so, it's Onwards and Upwards and all of that kind of stuff. Left only with the proverbial, 'shove off the cliff,' to blame.

"Where will you be going?" she had asked Vanessa conversationally, who, objecting to her cheery manner promptly spat back, "You think I'd tell you, you think I'd tell any of you?" throwing her a filthy sideways glance as she continued with packing her boxes, one on top of the other.

The Koins, standing in the doorway of the office, were watching the progress of the slowly filling trailer, determined to see no last minute disruptions to the peace. Vanessa, looking over at them, yelled, "You'll get yours, you wait and see!" nodding her head knowingly.

Mr Koin responding, a small warning sounding in his tone, "That's enough of all that, there is no need for all that carry-on!"

He leant back on the brick wall of the Office, his aged arms riddled with large veins, were folded across his chest. Looking out from under the rim of his sunhat, his scrawny, ancient, overly tall frame was relaxed, his dismissal of her already apparent. His brittle look, as he watched their busy efforts, was one of determined defiance and an unmistakeable statement to Vanessa, telling her he was not going anywhere until after she was long gone, and only a thing of the past. Mrs Koin, saying nothing, only looked at Vanessa with a look that said 'hopeless.' And, with a shake of her head before going back inside the Office, to sit at the desk and watch from there, occasionally saying something to Mr Koin, who turned his head toward her and nodded his reply.

Deciding this was a battle she wanted no part of, and giving up on any civility from Vanessa, she said, "Well, good luck to you, Vanessa, hope all goes well for you both," and she started to walk away, aware as she did so, that Vanessa had ignored her, only continuing with the unwelcome chore of loading her belongings onto the slowly filling trailer.

Her friend, carrying things down the stairs for her to pack onto the trailer, took no notice of anyone and kept about his business. His impatience to get out of there was obvious in the speed he ran up and down the high stairs with, often taking two at a time.

Three weeks later, she was returning to her unit when she stopped to chat with the group of youngsters lounging around one of the outdoor tables, having a beer or two (or three) after a hard day at it, all of them looking sweaty and dirty. Bronzed and tired out from their outdoor line of work, the summer sun vicious at this time of the year.

"Did you hear about the break-in?" one of them had asked her, almost casually. Tiredness, subduing any previously felt excitement for this latest casualty to Law and Order.

"No!?" she replied questioningly, choosing to stay standing, keen to be on her way and not wanting to appear as if she had the time to hang about with them.

"Yeah, up at the Koins cottage," he said, managing a grin as he looked down at the beloved coldie cradled between his nurturing hands.

A few of them talking at once, said, "A couple of nights ago. Remember, when the Koins were away for a few days?" not waiting for her to respond, they went on. "Amazed, you didn't see the Police here!" another followed.

"I've been using the side entrance lately," she replied dismissively, not offering any more personal details than that. Her ambiguity was becoming a habit, and coming far too naturally to her of late. "Have been a bit busy and always in a hurry lately. Haven't really seen anyone," she said, carefully excluding the fact this long standing avoidance had always been on purpose.

The youngsters looked around at each other, some laughing, some tiredly shrugging.

"Three guesses as to who's behind it, I reckon!" one of them finally stated, only saying what the others had wanted to.

"Yeah, she'd have it in her, that's for sure, and with her habits, she knows a lot of the right people too," another one finished for him.

There was no need to name any names. On reflection, a fair few had been waiting for something like this to happen.

Vanessa had never been known to walk away, defeated. Her tenacity to hold on, was an unbelievably, unmoveable trait. Her reputation as someone not to make an enemy of had been well earned.

"Do they think she is behind it?" she asked, "be a bit obvious, wouldn't it?" she added.

"They'd have to think that, wouldn't they? And I think 'obvious' would suit Vanessa, you know, the message she wants them to get!" someone speculated. "She always was a bit of a Boss-boy."

They were quiet for a moment, looking at each other. One of them finally said, "We haven't said anything to anyone, not interested in talking to the Cops so you be quiet about it, but a few of us think we saw them at it."

Another one, busting to be included in this secret they all shared, and talking over everyone else, went on, nodding his head vigorously, "Hmmm, yep. It was about one o'clock in the morning, there was two of them doing something at the back window of the Koins cottage!"

Someone else continued for him, "We were on our way over to the All Night shop, up on Main Street. They took off when they saw us coming, so we took no notice."

Another one said with open honesty, laughing, "Well, I wasn't going to get involved, anyway! Not that bloody stupid, hey!? Are you!?" he asked, looking at the other fellow who had been speaking. "They must've come back, because they got in. Either that, or we saw them coming out."

She asked, more concerned for Vanessa than curious for the Koins loss, "Much taken?"

They laughed. "Don't know, we've been staying clear. Besides, we'll get to hear all about it soon enough I reckon, you know how it goes around here!"

They all murmured their agreements, in this. They sure did know how it goes around here.

She said her goodbyes, again promising they could count on her silence and continued onto her unit, knowing it was only a matter of time before they would all be approached to answer some well-directed questions. All par for the course, no one would be excluded. A few days later, she was passing the little Office when Mrs Koin, poking her head outside the door, asked would she mind coming inside, if she had a spare minute or two.

"Sure," she said, knowing full well what this was going to be about. Just a little interested herself anyway, and keen to get it over and done with. Sometimes, the Horse's Mouth is the only way to go.

The quizzing of everyone was a normal event whenever anything occurred around the place, so she might as well have it done with, and put behind her. It could be expected by all the people who not only lived there, but the regulars who came and went, also. Mr and Mrs Koin knew them all. Anyone, who appeared on the grounds too often, would have been checked out as standard policy, their curiosity about everyone was typical, and not only for any half-hearted security reasons.

"Did you hear about the break-in?" Mrs Koin asked pointedly, not beating about the bush and getting right down to it.

She took a breath, tread carefully, she thought.

"Only just recently," she answered, "I've not been here so much lately." Amusingly, she felt a slight association to William with his, "I can't see anything!"

Mrs Koin continued on, as if she had not heard what she had said, "Do you know where Vanessa went off to?" her eyes sharp now, a frown on her forehead, looking up, she studied her.

She was well known for her time honed ability to see through you. If you were less than honest, it was a surety, more often than not. Either that, or people just giving themselves away by their apprehension and nervousness, and their belief of her doing just that, showing all over their demeanour. But she doubted it was just this alone, for she had seen the old woman in action before, and she really was quite formidable. Earning her a status for accuracy that was really quite fierce, and nevertheless, even the unbelievers believed.

By the sharpness of her question, this was definitely going to be a quizzing which would take in all of the residents in the very least, she knew. It was one battle Mrs Koin did not want to lose, either.

"No, I don't think she told any of us where she was going," she fended, then, "Did they get much?"

"Come and have look, I'll show you what they did," determinedly, Mrs Koin said over her shoulder, already turning away toward the connecting door leading inside, above which was a sign in large letters saying, PRIVATE.

She followed her, thinking, 'Here goes…. the Inner Sanctum!'

They continued on through. Passing a private Office into a lounge room and on into the kitchen, to stand before the rickety back door with its' paint peeling and chipped. Small paint flakes scattered onto the floor, to lie there, seemingly unnoticed by the old woman, now fussing her way towards the little window set oddly into the back wall.

Appearing more stooped than usual, her gait almost dragging, the recent stress taking its' toll. Her hair newly coloured in the dark, glossy brown which covered the grey completely. The colour, always the favoured one she had used for quite some years now, with her regular weekly appointment at her Hair Dresser showing a successful new trim, as well. She looked manicured and well kept, as was her usual way, and still looking ten years younger than she really was. She had been heard often, telling someone, "God still keeps me nice."

She had never been into the 'Inner Sanctum' before, and her absorption was distracting. Yes, she had been as far as the back door before, after a Sunday Service when delivering dirty dishes from the little Chapel behind the Cottage, but never had she come inside. She looked around at the general chaos.

The lounge room showing off years and years of objects collected, then left where they had first been placed. Books, all religious in their content lay strewn over surfaces everywhere. A television angled into one corner. Two big, dirty, brown vinyl reclining chairs, covered in a multitude of cracks, set side by side. A small table, stacked full of piles of books, was placed comfortably between them. The chairs, left in their extended positions and permanently facing the television, were the only main feature in the little cramped room.

There were layers of dust over everything, except the two big chairs. The constant use ensuring their lack of dust, although, even they had great thick cobwebs hanging beneath them and amongst the mechanics which controlled their movements. Everywhere, there was that 'old persons' smell that well used homes of the aged, seemed to get.

She realised Mrs Koin was still speaking to her, had needed to repeat herself a few times, and she forced her attention back to the little window beside the rear door, which Mrs Koin, now intent on, was pointing to. She gathered herself up and forced herself back into the present.

"See this broken catch here, that's how they got in," Mrs Koin was saying. "They broke the catch, and then they forced it open," she said, with some regret at not having repaired it when they should've, the 'it'll be right!' pushed too far.

She examined the small catch Mrs Koin was showing her. It did not take much of an examination to see how useless it was. "It's a bit flimsy, isn't it? How did they fit through that little window?" she asked the old woman, her half listening still blatantly showing.

With an exasperated sigh, a lack of patience, and an annoyed look thrown at her, Mrs Koin answered, "They stuck their hand through and opened the back door!" she demonstrated, frustrated with her distracted and absent-minded audience.

She continued, "The Police said we should have had better security on this window, the catch wasn't good enough. They were surprised we hadn't had trouble before this," she said with casual honesty and unusual self-reproach.

She saw that other than the broken catch, there appeared to be no other damage done and said, "Looks like it was easy for them, did they get anything of value?"

The old woman shook her head, her tiredness from the overly drawn out stress beginning to show.

"No, we don't keep cash here. They just pulled everything apart looking for things, broke the locks on the desk drawers in our Office. They took a new bottle of After Shave the grandkids gave Mr Koin for his birthday and broke a few things, but that's all."

Mrs Koin smiled, "We should take notice of anyone smelling nice, hey?" trying one of her odd attempts at humour, and slightly off the mark as usual.

She put a hand lightly on the old woman's shoulder, avoiding too much familiarity. "Well, at least that's something, isn't it?" she replied, not knowing what to say and edging towards the back door.

That 'old person' smell threatening to overwhelm her, encouraging her in her passage towards the sunshine and fresh air outside. She also suspected, that the shattered window was not the only gift left for the ancient occupants, the smell of urine permeated the rooms, as well. Her feeling of nausea was borderlining again with just the thought of them living amongst it.

"Let me know if I can do anything," she said quickly, looking for a way to make a faster exit.

"The Police are looking for Vanessa. They want to speak to her and I'm sure they will find her, but if you hear where she might be, can you let us know?" Mrs Koin asked, as she followed her out to the rear entrance and sunshine. Unconcerned for the directness of her request and purposefully sounding her demand, her eyebrows raised in support, eyes hard, in her expectation of the anticipated assurances.

"Sure, but I doubt she told anyone anything. She made sure of that. See you later then," she replied cheerfully as she kept walking toward the street.

Lifting a hand to wave behind her, as she quickly went. Not wanting to give the old woman time to ask questions about what she might've heard, in the form of local gossip. A question she had been surprised was not asked straight up, only Mrs Koins' tiredness saving her the awkwardness.

Silly girl. I hope it was worth it to her, this resolute 'having the final word,' she thought as she walked. Even if she has not signed a new Lease Agreement somewhere, nor paid a Bond wherever she had gone off to, the Police would still find her. Vanessa was a single mum, on a Supporting Parent Pension. She knew the Police had the authority to apply to the necessary Government Departments to release information to them, such as a current address. It would be easy and instant, for them. They would have it in no time, at all.

Still, if they could not prove her connection, she would be free and clear, and her point made.

She was certainly game enough to try such a thing on. Vanity, and the belief in her own invincibility, was a product of the constant use of Speed, as was her enduring rage. All of this, was well supported by her 'take no prisoners' personality.

As it went, she had covered a good deal of all the bases, especially the one that had her elsewhere at the time of the break-in, conveniently spending a night or two with distant relatives.

The two men involved in the burglary would never be caught, either.

THE GREAT BRAWL

The Great Brawl had been waggishly named by a few of the facetious lads about the Complex, who were more than just a little peeved. They had not been home at the time of this impromptu party and therefore, had missed out on all the action, much to their ire. A good punch up, for right or wrong, was something any red blooded Aussie bloke enjoyed thoroughly and loved to get amongst, especially those under the age of thirty. Growing tired of the way in which a darned old fashioned fist to cuffs, had become a serious riot in the retelling of the tale by those involved, just like those big fish stories every fisherman seems to have in the multitude, they had come to laugh amongst themselves with someone saying, "What? You mean the great brawl?" and the affectionate and flippant term, had stuck.

What had begun as four or five of the fellows, getting together for a few drinks out on the verandah on a Saturday afternoon off, grew into a crowd of forty or fifty, then more. People milling around with the drinks aplenty enjoying themselves, and romping raucously and happily about. By nightfall, the volume of noise was not the only thing that was escalating. The comings and goings had also increased, with cars parking wherever they could squeeze in. Losing count of the amount of people milling around between cars and wherever they could find ground space to stand on, the local inhabitants watching on, had begun to feel uneasy with the expanding and unfamiliar crowds.

The Party had started.

Groups of young people, the boys showing their youth and modern styling more so by their hair-do than their clothing, and the girls in their short dresses and very high heels, looked somewhat out of place and were definitely not the usual patronage you would ever see about Koins Motel. Some of the girls complaining about the difficulty such heels made for standing constantly on broken and cracked concrete, an ankle or two already paying the price. All of them looked very young, and they were full of life in the way only known by the younger set.

The knock-on effect of one invites one, invites one, all started by a few couples' knowing one the blokes who lived there and then others responding to their casually made invitation to call in too, was having its' success on the numbers now arriving in a continual stream. A modern day phenomena, and a consequence of easy communications.

All of this overcrowding was only made possible by the regular annual sabbatical of the Koins and their family. This time, across the seas once again to Egypt and their beloved Holy Lands. Their absence leaving the way clear for a little letting the hair down and party time, for those so inclined to make use of their time away.

The din of enthusiastic conversation rose and fell. A constant buzz, then sometimes louder and rising above the loudly playing music someone had tuned in, on a rather tinny sounding radio. Everything had been on a reasonable and acceptable level for some hours, and the tenants who had chosen not to attend had begun to take no notice of the continued proceedings, growing bored with watching the people milling about, talking.

This all changed rather quickly, and some said later, "Dam it! That's what happens the moment you stop watching. The pot boils over!"

Once started, this pot boiled over quickly, and no one could stop it. The yelling voices were the first alert that something was up, followed by the sounds of crunching, scraping metal, as someone picked up a metal fold-up chair and threw it at a parked car.

Choosing to stay in front of the telly and distancing herself from the crowds outside, finally, hearing the voices of two or three people yelling at each other above the din of the crowd, and taking only a moment to decide she still could not be bothered moving. Thinking about the size of the crowd outside, it was inevitable there would be a few noisy altercations after all, and not worth forfeiting the comfort of a large and cosy armchair over.

Unable to make out any of the content of the screamed exchanges and not really wanting to try, she nonetheless thought again, this was always going to be a given. When you add hours of uncontrolled boozing and a large number of people together, someone was bound to have a falling out, and things always go askew. When you put the younger generation together with a slightly older set too, you can bet something was going to give. Especially, since it is a time old honoured tradition and a historical fact, that generational change sets the bar for discourse and excludes no one from these differences, no matter how good the intentions. How otherwise, can you achieve progress?

The, "G'day old man!" say's the twenty year old to the thirty year old, is a perfectly normal and acceptable perception, and experienced by every generation for centuries long past.

Everyone takes their turn at both sides of this sliding scale. Putting both of these things together, with all of those combinations, it looked like a hotbed you would never be able to control, to her. An event perfectly moulded to furnish a hell of a fireworks display.

So, she continued to show no interest in the goings on outside, diligently trying to ignore it all. When the noise began to rise above the volume of the telly, when she could no longer concentrate on the programme she had been watching, she arose from her chair. Leaving the light off, she went to the window, drawing the curtain aside, she looked towards the now growing melee outside.

She was surprised to see how the crowd of people attending had grown by such a large proportion, since she had last taken any notice. How, their cars were now parked in the seemingly available car parks of other tenants' empty garages, as well as lining the driveways both in and out. She knew how pleased some of them would be to discover their pilfered spots on returning home later that night, and their inability to drive in at all.

She could see a small group of arguing people at the centre of the watching crowd surrounding them. Their arms with closed fists waving at each other, faces contorting with the verbal vitriol they were throwing at each other in their escalating efforts and rising tensions. The bulk of the crowd, still relaxing in general party mode, were not taking it all too seriously, yet. Some were yelling support for some, opposition to others. Some laughed and yelled their comments, enjoying their time out. Others spurred the aggressive ones on, and some called for calm. There were those that were trying to intercede between the arguing groups and calling for rationale. Then there were others who were taking no notice at all, still wrapped up in their own company and completely unaware of the growing unease around them, or the jostling they were taking as others pushed up against them.

THE GREAT BRAWL

It was when someone picked up a heavy outdoor chair, meaning to throw it at the one they were arguing with, instead, hitting a big glass sliding door, cracking and splintering it in every direction, that the fun and games really began and all prospects of reason and calm, went out the door.

For a moment, everyone froze as they were, silence descending for a second, then realising it was on, erupting in noisy confusion all at once. Even those only interested in their own company, their conversations slowing now, took interest in what was going on around them.

The crowd moved as one great wave. Those, uninterested in any quarrels were caught up anyway and swept away as one, with the rest of the moving mob. Their loud protesting's to their plight, mistakenly appearing at first to any observers, to be a support and encouragement for a more hostile involvement. All, seemingly knowing their sides of alliance, they turned on each other.

In the midst of it all, a figure who had been clipped by the sailing outdoor chair, on its' way towards the glass door, rolled around on his back on the ground, firmly clasping a raised knee and screaming loudly, feeling his pain. The broken sounds of wailing only feeding the crowd, compelling them on. It was when someone in the small inner circle threw a connecting punch, that the argument erupted into a full on fight, with everyone instantly involved. Pack mentality, demonstrated at its' most effective of moments.

Punches back and forth, people falling to the ground, the fighting began to spread outward, like the ripples of a stone thrown into a pond would do. And just as quickly.

Some, picking up chairs or whatever the furniture was around them, threw them in any direction they could, caught up now in the participation of a good fight only, and with no forethought for any chosen or unintended victims alike.

The noise of crunching metal and breaking windscreens loud in the night, melding with the sounds of splintering glass as doors and windows were smashed and cracked, impartially. People were falling to the ground, others picking themselves up. Blood rolling down faces and dripping onto clothing, leaving unmistakable dark splotches on the paler coloured T-shirts and clothing, adding to the ghoulish and frightening effect.

They exploited anything they could find as usable weapons. Picking up lumps of wood, branches lying in garden beds, larger stones and the outdoor furniture close by, all of it soon became dangerous flying projectiles. The tools of choice, by insane and unthinking people.

Bottles that so recently had been held in celebrating hands now became handy weapons. Wielded with relish and rising delight, smashing them over heads and throwing them in random directions. Some connecting and others crashing, broken, on bitumen driveways and concrete floored verandahs.

Females, screaming and screeching, with some running back down the driveways and out towards the open road, trying to escape injury and any unwanted involvement, terrified of personal harm. Others, choosing to join in the fight and giving every bit as good as the men. Those expensive, unbelievably high heels becoming severe weapons of preference, and causing far more serious injury than the comical image of women flailing about, shoes in hand, might otherwise have portrayed.

There were people jumping on car bonnets and roofs, intending damage. Others, on top of cars, slipping and sliding about in their hasty climb, were trying to get above it all, anxious to find any sort of relative safety on offer.

Some, hanging over opponents backs with arms locked around their necks, their victims desperately trying to release these false embraces. Others, carting someone around on their back as if in some odd game of Leap Frog gone wrong.

All over, there were bodies lying about, and growing in prostrate numbers by the minute. Some, not moving and some groaning, in their painful attempt to get up off the ground. Others, being tripped over and trodden on by the still able Soldiers in the continuing war all around them. Everywhere, was bloodied and bruised people, dinted cars and smashed glass, with broken and over-turned furniture lying topsy-turvy amongst it all.

A single lost, impossibly high heeled shoe lay on its' side, blood on the pointed heel leaving ominous implications in it's' wake, a grizzly confirmation of the intensity of the violence before.

By the time the Police cars rolled into the Complex, all of the witnessing tenants who had not been participants, deciding it was now safe to come out, were helping those lying about, or were picking their way through the carnage, careful of the broken glass on the ground around them and strewn all about, especially the hidden clumps of sharp things under ripped branches and other broken bits and things.

Many of the combatants, who could still help themselves, had fled the scene before the impending Police troops could gather them up. Those, who could get into cars not blocked in, had taken them and ran for it, and they would be the only ones who may have got away, unimpeded. Others, just left their cars there. Running, when they heard the sirens, to be picked up later by the Police, their details obtained from the Registrations of their deserted cars.

All those who had witnessed the exhibition, were shocked and disbelieving at how fast the amicable gathering had turned into one of such destruction and violence. And, it would be just something else to be added to the local hazardous reputation of Koins Motel. The devastation, now looking far worse in the aftermath than the fight itself had appeared to be, was going to be quite something for the clean-up crews to deal with.

After the ambulances had loaded their cargo and left for their prospective destinations, after the Police had taken their statements and had spoken to everyone they could, while Forensics ploughed through the wreckage, the tenants who had helped out as best they could, gathered together to watch on, finding comfort in the familiarity of each other, while the last of it was sorted by those now in charge.

'The Great Brawl,' it was said later, by someone who had been more persistent and successful in their probing of the Police in attendance, had all begun when someone had refused to share their cans of Jim Beam rum and coke with another, whose supply had simply ran out.

JIMMY

The pair hunched over the cage in the backyard, had been there since early that morning. They had been arguing, or, as they would have it, healthily discussing, everything from where to put it, what direction would be best, and then, how to leave the bait. Now, they seemed to be having some trouble figuring out how to set the trapdoor.

They had already decided it did not matter what food they left as bait. The wild cats the scruffy pair in the backyard was trying to catch were starving hungry and would eat anything they left out, but it had still taken a discussion of some fifteen minutes or so, before they had arrived at this simple conclusion. Dumb and dumber were this pair, and the whole scene so far, had been one of continued hilarity. The entertaining side to a sober intent, a welcome reprieve at least.

At first, she had been concerned about them setting a trap up behind her unit. After giving it some time to develop, she concluded she would see to it nothing came of it anyway, and gave them all the time they wanted to enjoy this, what was turning out to be, hard to achieve endeavour that they had set themselves about, so enthusiastically. The concentration and seriousness it had taken, you'd have thought they were solving the problems of World Policies.

At least the rest of the nearby neighbours were getting a good laugh out of it all, their lack of ability a sight for all, and unsurprising to any of them. They were not a pairing you would give any responsibilities to, not if you had any common sense at all.

Every unit had their own little family group of wild cats who had adopted them. The cats, seeming to respect each other's turf, never strayed onto another's territory. This behaviour was probably a consequence of such a huge amount of them, and with every litter, their numbers growing tenfold because of the amount of females born and how soon they too, could give birth. They co-operated with each other, in order to survive.

None of them had been spayed. Not even the Council, whose central Offices were opposite the Complex, considered them, or had any approach to limiting their numbers other than to Catch and Kill. Their best effort appeared to be one of, 'let's just ignore them and they might go away.' The poor little things were the ones to suffer for this lack of interest and everyone tried, as best they could, to look after the little group that had chosen them and their back door, as their home ground.

She had a mother and four little ones that stayed under the bushes by her back door. Every night she made sure she had some scraps to throw out for them. They dashed out to grab at everything she put there, looking up at her as they darted back under cover, not ever staying out in the open for very long at any time.

They remained wild, never allowing anyone to get close or approach them, but she knew they looked for her every evening, waiting expectantly, for her to place her little bowls down, and they considered her with appreciation for her existence in their lives.

She had no idea what sex her little four were. You could not get close enough to them for that inspection, but she did know the babies were thriving and growing into healthy looking young cats. Thanks only, to her dedication to them getting a feed and a large bowl of milk every day.

She worried what would become of them, when she had moved on and was no longer there to tend to them. She put the thought out of her mind as soon as she had it. She was not game to think about or extend any concern, to the hundreds of others about the Complex. Choosing to limit such thoughts to her five was something she could cope with, and her bit of aid done. The emotional drag was too much otherwise, no one could carry the world on their back, no matter how much they wanted to.

Starvation may have been the main problem for the cats to contend with, but it was not the only threat to them they lived with daily. The five acres of the bushy, treed surrounds of the Complex provided a haven in the midst of this busy tourist Town, for a large number of Carpet Snakes. The suitably tropical environment made even more ideal, by the seemingly unlimited amount of food the cats provided for them, and their total had grown considerably over time.

The snakes naturally grew to a massive size, but since they posed no threat to mankind and indeed, were used in many tropical places, where they would be placed into ceiling spaces to keep the mice and rats down, no one seemed to take much notice of them about the Complex. Unless they trespassed too close to home and then they would be given short shrift quickly, back to the leafy confines of the yard, to hide amongst the overgrown foliage, once again.

There had been a few times she had stood at the kitchen sink, looking out into the back garden, in time to see a great snake in the process of swallowing an unwitting cat. The huge lump slowly working its' way down the snakes length.

Since they strangled the animal first, she knew the cat had felt no real pain. Still, it was an unnerving sight and was one she always looked away from. She reconciled herself with the truth that it was only the old and infirmed the snakes caught up with anyway. In their slow moving way, they provided a sort of a service and decaying dead animals were never seen about the grounds very often.

The mother cats seemed to be experts in keeping their newborns away from the snakes, although she often wondered how. It was one of those curiosities of the wild, and the cats were certainly as crafty and courageous as any wild animal anywhere.

Turning her attention back to the two men fiddling about the back garden, their banter an odd form of verbal tennis, back and forth, back and forth, then, jubilance at a point scored. She stifled a laugh.

One of the young men leaning over the cage was Mickie, and her workmate from the strawberry fields, he had been responsible for bringing her here, in the first place. She knew he did not have a lot upstairs but she had, only since living so near to him, found that this was a young man with a troubled mind and a troubled life, and hence, a troubled past.

He was a fussing, abrupt and often confused man, whose strange interpretations of religion had led him finally, to a Community Church that was all gospel singing, with an American Evangelistic approach to their gatherings. Encouraging everyone to bring their families into their fold, and that to put them under their complete guidance was also an important part of their regime. He somehow, always managed to get into an argument with Mr Koin over his particular ways of celebrating his faith, and he had long since stopped his occasional attendances to the Sunday lunches at Deliverance Hall, as a form of his personal protest. That, along with the constant harrying of

Mr Koins' convictions upon him, was too much for him to suffer and a burden to his fragile health.

He was registered as suffering a mental condition by the appropriate Government Departments, after a long, drawn out dispute in the Courts with his ex-Wife. Subsequently, he could only see his two young sons on the rare predetermined dates chosen by her, and always chaperoned by an outside Social Worker on these infrequent occasions. Something he railed against vigorously, with him swearing to continue his fight, no matter what, but never really doing anything about it. There would never to be a time when he was allowed to take his young sons out on an excursion somewhere, only seeing them for an hour at most, with them sitting at the table outside of his unit.

He could often be seen, with his cleaning bits and pieces, striding like a little tin soldier, arms swinging, along the main street, on his way to some window cleaning job one of the local Business owners had given him to do, more out of sympathy, than their need for the work to be done. At other times, he would push his hand mower around the streets, offering to cut the lawn of any unsuspecting person he would find outdoors as he passed by. More often than not, doing the work for only a few dollars or nothing at all, depending on how much in needy circumstances he judged them to be, or how well he had liked them.

The Business owners all knew of Mickie's circumstances, even though he often filled his days knocking on their doors, asking for work in such a way as to represent himself as an independent and self-employed Cleaner. They ignored the lack of truth in this and most of them gave him what time they could, their kindness and compassion obvious for all to see. For those he did not know well, or who were new to the area, he would claim to be the Supportive Parent of two young boys, finding that this line of approach was often more successful, than not. His mental abilities being what they were, it never occurred to him that this misrepresentation would one day go against him, after word had inevitably and innocently spread, the Business owners knowing each other fairly well in this small enough, tourist Town. But, that was Mickie for you.

She believed he did all of this running about, speaking with anyone he could, out of loneliness more than his need for any supplementary income. And, she was sure the people he spoke to at these times, could recognise this fact, also.

This morning, he had finally decided to take a stand against what he called 'the Koins' breeding of wild cats,' and he had said as much to the poor woman who had served him at the Counter of the Council offices earlier, when picking up the cage that he and his helper were now trying to set. He had paid for only one since they were $2.50 each for a twenty four hour hire.

How, he thought a single cage, which would go off when only one cat had entered it, after following the tantalising smell of left food, would make any difference in the number of the hundreds of cats which scampered under the bushes, everywhere around the five acre Complex, she did not know. The protest it represented seemed to pacify him and settled his complaints, for the moment.

He had put a lot of thought into what effort he might offer up. Going over all sorts of ideas for months and months, his Christian guidelines impelling him to, do something. The more his thoughts were fruitless with no real solutions coming, the more bothered and aggravated he became, entering the boundaries of an obsession. It became a larger than life cause, one that he had to see to, if he was to ever stop his mind from whirring, round and round. The anguish of seeing them at feed times every evening, only caused him physical pain. Eventually, he had found himself at the counter of the Council offices, where he had finally sought their advice on what he could do to help. Little did they know when suggesting trapping them, that in his mind, one trap would move mountains.

Jimmy, his unusual companion in this enterprise, was a young twenty two year old country boy. His only real ambition in life was to sit in front of his screen, playing his nonstop video games and staying permanently stoned. Leaving his unit only when he had to find some way to replenish his stash, which he did begrudgingly, by many and varied means.

He was well educated by parents who were Primary School teachers, but he was possibly their most unsuccessful student. Rejecting anything that looked like hard work, or which might take any effort at all. He was one of those people who seemed to be born with a natural allergy to work, cold shivers making his skin crawl at the mere mention of it, even though the effort it took to avoid it could be more than any effort the job may have taken in the first place, and with no monetary rewards at the end of it all.

A few had tried to convince him to give the strawberry fields a go during the last Season but were always rewarded with the same reply of, "that's hard work, isn't it?" with a wry grin to follow. In fact, this country boy had managed to never have had a paying job since leaving High School, and he was proud of it. He was an adept at getting around the Advisors at the Social Security Office, and he had been on Unemployment Benefits for years now.

There were those who wished they knew his secret, as Unemployment Benefits came with all sorts of personal input requirements that the under thirties had to comply with. He knew the system well and he had the gift of the gab, there was no doubting it, his lifestyle was proof enough of this.

Watching them, she surmised that Mickie, who was a known supporter of those in need and an easy touch for the cunning, must be paying him ten dollars in cash to gain his aid now. Although, aid, appeared to be an ill used expression for what was going on outside.

She remembered the time Jimmy's parents had come for a quick drop-in visit, on their way home to the country from a holiday spent somewhere else. How, he had chased their car out of the driveway and up the road as they were leaving, waving wildly and yelling his goodbyes. How the sad look in his mothers' eyes, as she had surveyed his surroundings, told the tale of her lost hopes. Fortunate for them, that they had three other grown and ambitious children they could put their pride in, she supposed.

He had come back smiling, panting from the car chase, waving the fifty dollar note his mother had pressed into his hand, and saying how good it was to see them. His enthusiasm spurred on by her generosity, even though he had refused to go on this annual holiday with them all, preferring not to give up his twenty four hour use of grass, or his nonstop video games. None of which, they knew of.

There was a very young pair of teenagers, a boy and a girl of around sixteen or so, who often came to visit with Jimmy, their loud laughter alerting everyone to their presence. They rode their bicycles in and propped them against the outside wall while they went inside, closing the door behind them.

They looked like any young group who were enjoying some involved video game together, and no one gave any real thought to them. That is, until the day an argument broke out momentarily, before Jimmy, having given them twenty five dollars to score for him, had to accept their claims that they had been busted before they could buy his grass for him. Jimmy was now out of pocket for a precious and 'hard earnt,' twenty five dollars.

Everyone knew of this, not because of overhearing any argument, but because Jimmy himself asked everyone around him if this sounded like it could be a true story, and did they think it really could have happened that way, or was he being taken for a ride, or being gullible, and what should he do about it? He seemed to think that any reassurances from others might make it alright. He sought the opinion of everyone he came across for a time, much to the indignation of some and earning a few astonished glances his way. Some of the less patient, older, road hardened gents just telling him to, 'Piss off, you bloody idiot!'

This little team of three had more than a few tricks up their sleeves, and were well-versed and well-practised in all of them. They embarked on these endeavours with their wholehearted enjoyment of the adventure and mischievousness of it all. The kinds of mischief only teenagers seem to think of. Their antics growing with their confidence, and finally, as antics that grow are likely to do, their final scheme turned into pure illegality, and as such, landed them all before the Courts.

The Complex was within walking distance to the Municipal Library which serviced the entire Town. It was a large, modern Library with facilities catering to every age and to all needs. Apart from a huge selection of books and videos from every genre, there were Services offering free internet and the free use of the computers. Needing only to book ahead, for a maximum of two hours use at a time, it was popular with all ages and many students. Free classes and training available for those in need of assistance in the use of the internet and the computers, with a separate section for the children, no one was left out. It was a hub of activity and constantly busy, their little car park was always full with the frequent comings and goings. All of this was set in lovely parkland surroundings.

The little group of three had begun making regular visits, strolling together in idle chatter and occasional laughter as they crossed the roads on their way to the Library, looking for the world like an innocent group of youngster, out to enjoy their day. Anyone who saw them on these sojourns, had thought how good this pair was for Jimmy, disbelieving that anyone or anything could have inspired him once, to show such interest in a Library, of all things.

These little journeys had gone on for some time when one day, she had been taking a short cut home through the parkland, the pathway leading alongside the Library for quite some way. Out of the corner of her eye, through the bushes, she spotted Jimmy, who appeared to be standing, lazily waiting, at the rear section of the latticed outdoor patio and reading area. The large patio taking up most of the back half of the Library building, and an odd place to be standing, waiting, at the best of times. An even odder place for Jimmy to be, at any time.

This outdoor area was a part of the main building and was designed to allow those who wished to sit and read, the opportunity to do so in an enclosed but outdoors setting, amongst the surrounding gardens growing at the edge of the parkland. It was a place you could not get to unless you pushed your way through the undergrowth, no paths taking you along this stretch of the building.

She paused, considering if she should go and say hello to the young man. He was standing in one spot, scuffing a foot back and forth, head bowed to watch his progress with the line he seemed to be drawing in the loose dirt. Before she could make up her mind to walk across to him, he stooped quickly, putting a hand under the bottom railing of the latticed wall, he withdraw a large square object, shoved it under his arm, glanced around furtively, and without any more hesitation, he turned and quickly walked away.

Watching him through the trees and hanging branches, quietly murmuring, "Oh, Oh!" she looked around instinctively, to see if anyone else was about. Only a strolling couple, hand in hand, could be seen off in the distance, there was no one else to witness this questionable gesture. She did not move for a time, taking a good look at the scene before her. How, the bushes and trees grew thickly around the lovely latticed verandah as it jutted out into its' leafy surrounds. The quietness and solitude of this section of the Library, perfect for the purpose it was designed for, and apparently, with a small flaw. A convenient flaw, for those with such an illegal agenda.

She could see that Jimmy had already disappeared, hidden by the bushy landscape, and she slowly and thoughtfully, set out in the direction of home. The same direction Jimmy had hurriedly headed for, so recently.

Days later, taking some time to herself, sitting outside at her table and sipping her coffee, she nodded at the figure of Jimmy as he came strolling through the side entrance. Seeing her sitting on her own, he came straight to her table and without feeling any need for an invitation, he sat down opposite her.

"I haven't seen you in ages," he said, as he sat down. A crooked smile turning the corners of his mouth up, almost but not quite, a sneer.

Saying nothing, she watched him settle in opposite her. He ignored her lack of enthusiasm, and the 'Hello' that did not come. He had grown familiar with indifferent welcomes, and he disregarded them like water off a duck's back. It was impossible to discourage him, if it suited him otherwise.

"Where have you been?" he persisted, not looking at her, his eyes scanning the Complex around them. This form of confidant dismissal was his usual custom, and she did not take it personally.

"Same as always, just coming and going," she answered with a shrug, without any commitment and maintaining her usual distance from the country boy who she had always found to be a bit of a trouble maker and a serious smart arse, definitely not one to be trusted alone in your unit, if you did not want to lose any pocket sized belongings, or valued little things.

Deciding she would throw her usual caution, and her lack of interest in him, to the wind this time, she told him rather directly, "You may not have seen me lately but I've seen you, Jimmy. What have you been up to at the Library?"

Choosing to do this, more so for his young age than any sense of right or wrong she may have had, and certainly not for any love for this directionless young smart bum. He stopped mid-sentence, his hands mid-air, this time looking straight at her.

"Why?" he asked, uncertainty clear in his voice.

Answering him without any hesitation and a little offhandedly, she said, "I saw you at the back of the Library the other day, what were you up to? What was the package you picked up?" She continued swiftly, not waiting for his response, "I saw you but you didn't see me. What makes you think no one else was watching you, too?"

He grinned at her. At first, she thought he was not going to answer her questions, then vanity and the need to gloat overwhelmed him.

"You're not going to believe it!" he said, the laughter giving his sentence a lyrical touch.

There's something to be said for giving someone enough rope, so, she stayed quiet, watching him. Her look mirroring the seriousness of the topic. She was not going to let him downplay this one.

Encouraged by his own self-fascination, he went on, "One of us goes inside and gets a Car Manual from the shelf, then goes outside to read it on the verandah, and then, when no one is around, they leave it on the ground, just under the edge of the railing." He told her this matter-of-factly, a narration filled with an odd kind of pride.

He continued on, explaining their processes, enjoying the chance to boast, "One of us waits outside, and when no one is about, they pick it up!" This time, the laughter in his voice was clear.

"We take turns in it, so it's never the same one of us!" he finished, watching her, a small look of hope in his eyes. Hope, that she was both slightly shocked and a little impressed by his cunning.

She wasn't going to give him that one, that was for sure. Especially, since she considered the whole thing to be childish, and far from worth the risk for such small rewards.

"Why, do you do that?" she asked, completely confused now, her innocence and lack of knowledge of such things confounding her.

"Because, they are hard to get and worth twenty five dollars up at the Second-hand Book Store on Main street," he told her matter-of-factly, smiling sweetly and slightly patronizing her, as if he thought her befuddled brain was a product of her age. How otherwise, did she not get it?

"How many times do you do this? Aren't they suspicious at the Bookstore?" she asked him.

"No, they never ask any questions, but we are careful. We swap around who goes in to see them," he told her, his suspicious tone suggesting that now, she was only being dumb.

"And we always wait until it's a different attendant than the time before," he went on, trying to convince her now, or at least, help her understand how this all worked.

She shook her head slowly, telling him, "You're going to get caught Jimmy. You can't do something like this too often!" then adding, "They have cameras up all over the Library, it's only a matter of time before they connect the footage, and with all their stock on computer now, they will discover soon enough, that only the Car Manuals are going missing and they will look at that footage," she told him firmly, scoldingly, then adding as an afterthought, "You think they haven't come up against the likes of you, before? Don't kid yourself!"

Like she said, too high a risk for too little reward. Not even a relief to the boredom, would make this scam worthwhile.

Never a one for wanting to hear how imperfect his plans were, or how he was bound for failure, he shrugged at her, all of a sudden disinterested in the topic.

"It'll be alright. They haven't so far, have they!? We've been doing it for a while, you will see, they are too busy there," he said, certainty sounding more like bravado and more forced now, than real.

She smiled at him, "Jimmy, it is only a matter of time. When they do their next stocktake, it will be found out. You will see." Deciding on one last try, she persisted, slightly enjoying how uncomfortable he was becoming.

"If they aren't listed as 'out,' then they will know they have been stolen!" she continued. "You are just in denial. Too cocky for your own good. You had better stop it now or you'll get caught. It can't go any other way!" she scolded him, determined to have the last word and not to let him have his way. She wanted to see him give in to her.

Standing up, he shrugged his shoulders dismissively, smiled and said, "We'll be okay. See you later!" his tone defiant, his nose held a little higher, as he looked down at her.

Smiling at her own naughtiness, she watched him walking away, the cocky sway to his shoulders, hands in his pockets, a confidant smile on his face. He did not look back. Oh well, she had tried, her conscience was clear in that, at least. That was the way she would look at it, she had never really believed she could sway the young know-all, anyway.

Jimmy had the archetypal personality trait of ignoring what he did not want to see, especially, if it got in the way of what he wanted. Who knows, might do him good to find out he was another mortal being, just like the rest of the crowd. The pedestal he had put himself on, was nothing more than an illusion, and as illusions are apt to do, they disappear, since they do not exist in the first place. Makes for a very tenuous place to sit, and a very high place to fall from. The ground at the bottom of such a fall, is never soft.

His unpopularity was not because of any unattractive personality traits though, it had come about because he was a compulsive thief. He would pick up anything and put it into his pocket, if it was small enough. She had seen him do this many times before. No one was exempt from this behaviour, and there was no such thing as best friends where Jimmy was concerned. He would do this to Mickie five minutes after Mickie had lent him money, and he would think nothing of it. Such, was the nature of Jimmy. He was simply untrustworthy.

She saw his young friends waiting outside his door. They laughed together as they went inside, one of them glancing back at her with a glib grin. Putting it out of her mind, she finished her much needed coffee, and found solace in the fact that some things you could not change, and that really, it was not her concern, and even more honestly, she did not actually care about the eventual outcome, anyway. It did not matter how she had tried to, she just could not seem to like this young man. It would be some weeks before she saw him again.

Walking through the side entrance after a long day at work, she had been distracted by a co-worker who had walked alongside her on her own way up to the Main Street, and the date she had waiting for her at the local Pub. They had been chatting about nothing in general and having a good laugh about the unappreciated amorous antics of a new young male Supervisor, towards the younger female staff members. Her friend had been trying to convince her to come along with them for a night out at the Pub, and she had not noticed the Police car parked outside of Jimmy's unit until she was almost behind it, or the two Police Officers who were tapping at his door. Glancing back, she saw the boy and girl sitting forlornly, in the back seat of the car.

The moment she saw them, she knew what it would be all about. The day of reckoning had arrived by the look of it all, the account had become payable and due. She continued onto her unit, determined to take no interest in what she had wiped her hands of, and had always known, would be a sure bet.

Opening her glass front door, the familiar smell of the ancient carpet hit her senses as usual. Security, was always a more important issue than any comfort, when choosing between the two. The necessity of closing the place up tightly before going out on these hot days, the choice was still a no-brainer, and even more so, here at Koins Motel. Though lately, she was not so sure anymore. It had been so very hot and humid it was like walking back into an oven, and a smelly one at that, every time you came home. It was becoming an impossibly long process trying to cool it down again, once it had been opened up.

She was standing at her kitchen sink, the cold water running loudly while she dashed her face and neck with it then poured a small glass to drink, when she heard her name whispered through the louvered windows above the sink. Looking up, she saw Jimmy standing on tip toes outside, peering at her through the flywire and security grill.

Pointing his finger towards her back door, he whispered, "Open up, quickly, let me in!"

"No! What are you doing?" she demanded loudly.

"Pleeease! Pleeease!" he begged her, his whispered request sounding like a high pitched squeak.

"No! What are you doing?" she repeated.

"I'm hiding! Don't let them know I'm here," he told her desperately, with a touch of disbelief in her refusal to help him, now.

"Quickly, before they find me. Please! Let me in!" he whispered again, looking quickly around.

"No Jimmy, I'm not going to do that, you should know that. Go around and front up!" she told him, not wanting to be dragged into anything not of her doing, more so, than her disapproval of him and his wayward goings on.

"They will only come back, you can't avoid them!" she added firmly, "It will go better for you if you go and Man up!" she added, challengingly.

"No!" he said, exclaiming decisively and sounding like a disobedient child. Before she could respond any further, he ducked down low and moved on quickly at a crouch, up towards Mickie's unit at the far end of the Complex, where he disappeared out of her sight. She was not sure if he was aiming at Mickie or at the side entrance and out onto the street, but she was sure that in time, they were all bound to hear about it again, whether they wanted to or not.

There would be a few souls watching behind those drawn curtains, smiling broadly at this final accounting for the light fingered and all too cocky, Jimmy. Their animosity, for those that were not team players, united by the harshness of their environment, was shared equally and never withheld. The protocols of the down trodden, "Take your share in the trouble that's going, and never go back on your mate!" To break with these rules, would not be forgiven.

She did know, that whichever direction it had been, it would only be delaying the inevitability of them catching up with him. Unless, he chose to get onto a bus out of town, and did it soon.

They found Jimmy not too long after that. The Police had left their curt instructions with Buff the Caretaker that the moment he was seen to call them immediately, and Buff was always happy to be of service in any community matters. Such things where important, after all.

She was unsure of how harshly the Courts had ruled against the little group of three in the end, but Jimmy had kept his head down for a little while after that. Steering clear of anyone he saw, and trying to avoid the laughing jeers anyone tossed his way. One thing was for sure, he was not quite so self-assured anymore. The threat of real jail time if he offended again, would terrify the errant Jimmy. No more video games or pot. Unthinkable!

A Court Order telling them to stay away from each other, and choosing to stay on the straight and narrow, the teenage duo was never seen at the Complex again.

The arguing couple in the back garden, had finished their task of setting the trap for a wary but starving cat, the entertainment over for the day. Only Mickie remained, fussing with indecision, going about the business of putting water and food at the end of the now, well set, cage. He was looking none the worse for the morning of arguments with Jimmy, about the complexities of pinning a trapdoor back. Double checking and then checking again, his obsessive behaviour a fixation, and now accepted as a normal part of everything he did in his daily comings and goings.

The next morning she had arisen as the sun was just coming up over the horizon, a beautiful golden orange glow spreading against the still black sky, and the fresh smell of the growing morning slowly dispelling the cool night air. Raucous sounds of bellowing birds filling the air, as they tried to outdo each other in their morning greetings to the rising sun.

She went straight to the window over her sink, looking out into the back garden, she saw that the trap had indeed, gone off.

There was only one cat inside the cage, but it was one of her beautiful, half grown kittens. Her favourite in fact. He was a lovely, solid looking little fellow. A boy, she was certain, because of his angular masculine face, and she was not at all surprised to find it was him. He was the game one of the litter, and he had always been the leader of his little pack, assuming the responsibility of checking out the lay of the land before the others would follow, scampering faithfully behind him. They would be somewhere close by, watching the cage from the shadows, hiding themselves under nearby bushes and shrubs, helpless to help their little brother but not leaving him now.

She went quickly to her back door, opening it, she went out into her back garden. With hurried steps, she went directly to the cage. The little cat crouched at the far end, hissing up at her, watching her carefully.

"Shush, baby," she whispered to him, glancing around, checking for any impending interference that she might have to fight off, and prepared for a life-sacrificing defence, should one be necessary. Reaching over to grab the door she moved to the other end of the cage, leaving him with the confidence of a clear passage to make good his escape when she lifted the trapdoor up.

With no hesitation, he flew out of the cage and disappeared under the bushes by her back door, only the rustling noises and the shaking bushes to mark his speedy passage. Standing up she watched him go, a smile on her face for her clever, quick witted little fellow.

Later that day when she saw Mickie in the back garden, standing over the empty cage, scratching his head at the untethered, now closed door, she went to her back door and called to him.

"Mickie, I want you to know, I let him out!"

Mickie looked over at her, mouth open, he wavered. "Why did you do that? It's a waste of the $2.50 hire fee," he asked her, whinging, with a hint of seriousness in his voice. Momentarily, thinking how his small offering was now null and void.

"It was one of my kittens and I'm not having that!" she told him dismissively. "Do you have any idea what the Council would do with him, Mickie?" she asked, her tone demanding. She already knew his response to that.

"Well, they will…." he stammered, unsure of the answer that he had not really considered, until now.

"They are wild, Mickie. The Council people can't even handle them. They will give them a needle and put them down, without even getting them out of the cage!" she told him with knowledgeable certainty.

"Why, they don't find a way of adding something to some feed that would stop them from re-producing, I don't know!" she continued, "I guess they don't have anything like that, so they put them down!" Determined to get this point across, she went on, "Do you think they really care about a few wild cats, or do you think they might feel they have more important things to deal with? It's in the 'too hard basket' for them, so they do nothing."

"Well, we have to do something, don't we?" he asked her, his eyes still locked disappointedly, on the wasted, empty cage.

"And, how does one cage help change things here at Koins?" she asked him, determined to undermine any future ventures.

He watched her solemnly, his brown eyes big and round, his hands fiddling with a tie rope.

"I know, it is a problem, but not my babies! Okay?" she told him, more gently now.

"So, you take your cage, and your pointless effort, and you put it in your own backyard, not mine! It's only a game for you, something to occupy your time. All right!?" she said.

He watched her. Without saying anymore, he bent over, lifted the cage, turned and walked away. Reaching the edge of his garden path, he stopped, confused, he turned and opened his mouth to say something more, but she lifted her finger and shook her head slowly, at him. She would brook no more arguments from him, over this unsolvable matter of the wild cats.

She never saw him with his $2.50 a day cage again, having given up on this hopeless remedy once and for all, it seemed.

THE WOMAN IN THE FLORAL DRESS

There were a few outsiders who visited friends at the Complex often enough, to almost seem like tenants themselves. Their comings and goings were such daily events that nobody took any notice of them, familiarity breeding a disinterest, and with their first names known by so many, these outsiders took for granted their adopted by all, status.

One woman, had managed such a long standing attendance at the Complex so as to have more than a couple of ex-boyfriends amongst the residents, and she ambled in and out so often, there were a few new tenants who simply assumed she was one of their neighbours. She could often be found sitting outside at one of the tables with one of her previous loves, filling in an empty hour or so. Her amicable manner seeming to endear her to her ex's, and with no heartfelt grudges, they always had time for her.

One in particular, feeling sorry for her and her flighty ways, never turned her away. It seemed that a past love had turned to compassion and pity with the passing of time, with a profound understanding of her self-induced plight through his familiarity and experiences of their own past relationship. His protectiveness and concern for her over the new Beau she was flaunting lately, prompted him to warn her against him and his bad boy ways.

"But," she had replied, "He is twenty five, and gorgeous!"

"When did you last see anyone younger than forty five interested in me!?" she had declared, contrarily.

A true enough fact, that had not been for the want of trying on her behalf. Many of the young men who had appeared to be single, had walked away smiling from a flirty confrontation with her on more than one occasion. With amused glances back over their shoulders and a shake of the head, both flattered and embarrassed at the same time.

And so, the ex-boyfriend had withheld anymore comments from her. Only stating his concerns to any of the neighbours who showed any willingness to listen to him, no matter how slight that willingness was. His caring actions soothing his conscience somewhat, from dumping her previously when he too, could not keep up with her manic ways, and had grown exhausted from the journey.

"You will see, no good will come of this. They both like the drink too much. You will see!" he would say often enough for some to begin to doubt his sincerity or concern for her, sounding much more like sour grapes from these overly repeated warnings, to people whose interest was only one of curiosity and politeness. The old, 'me thinks he doeth protest too much!' becoming apparent.

She would arrive in some new pretty dress, always floral and generally strappy, with plenty of cleavage bared and helped by the push-up bra. Sandaled feet, showing off neatly painted red toes. Her short bobbed, bleached blonde hair, with the perpetual black roots always exposed.

When she met and pursued her latest beau, nobody could be bothered to consider the fact she was fifteen years older than the good looking but rebellious young man. In today's world, it was common enough, and no one really thought it was anything more than a passing fancy, especially for the young man, who found more than a little convenience in this new relationship.

The woman appeared to be around forty or so. It was hard to tell. The deep lines that crossed her heavily made-up face, were a penalty for the years of heavy drinking, and the boozing had aged her well before her time.

She had a ten year old daughter who she dragged with her everywhere she went, no matter what the time of day or night it might be. Everyone knew the little girl was her youngest one, and that she had others who were nineteen and older and no longer living with her, thankfully, out on their own, and solely governing their own destinies. All of them, off on their own great adventure that is the journey of life, stranding the little ten year old girl on her own, to contend with her drunken mother as best she could. For the most part, she contended very well, having the practise of her whole young life behind her to draw from, since she had not known anything else, really. That, combined with that great resilience of children.

In all the time the woman had been coming daily to the Complex, on her search for company to fill the lonely day, she had never yet been sober. Many, had passed disapproving comments to her driving in her constant state, especially when she had the little girl in the car with her, but she threw a grin at them and saying nothing else, ignored them all. Disapproving comments, were something she had coped with for a very long time and she had become hardened and immune to them. Discovering long ago, it was easier and less gruelling to simply ignore them. What was there to be said, after all? Excuses, only made the conversations and discussions longer anyway, adding more ammunition for these encounters to be repeated time and time again.

This new union had appeared to be a happy and welcome one in the beginning. Both the woman and the younger man came and went together, always laughing and joshing with each other. The younger man attentive, always taking the time to treat the little girl kindly whenever she was with them in their pursuits, which was most of the time.

This went on for a few months before cracks began to appear. The younger mans' annoyance and growing lack of patience, for his new partners' ability to consume all of the booze he could provide began to build daily, and it did not take long to show itself openly. Sensing the younger mans' attitude change, the woman began to display an unwillingness to pander continually, to the younger mans' needs, and over the course of a few weeks this tit-for-tat back and forth'ing grew obvious to the most casual of observers, the malice mounting with the passing of each day.

The minor arguments started when he no longer always answered the phone to her calls, and when he was no longer always available to take her somewhere, or to meet with her. In protest to his reluctance, she began to deny him her availability to drive him wherever he wanted to go, or to deliver his groceries or his drink to him.

The power-plays had begun, and the happy, laughing pair had slipped into a new daily routine.

At first, the visits amounted to nothing more than her showing up unexpectedly, when he did not answer his phone. She would sit quietly at his outside table and wait for him to either come out or come home. Talking with whomever she knew who went by, somehow, the conversations working their way around to questions of whether or not he had been seen with someone else lately, and leaving the recipients of her questionings, feeling uncomfortable and troubled.

Her concerns about being replaced by a younger woman were to be the natural progression for her insecurities, and finally, after coming to the fore, became the focus of all her thoughts. Astutely ignoring the complaints about her constant drinking, and with her practised ability to pretend it was not a cause or an issue, only frustrating anyone who took part, whether their involvement in any conversations with her was by choice or by force. Eventually, these unexpected visits would occur without the need of an unanswered phone call.

Her annoyance grew with every visit she made, and her demands on the younger man began to induce his rage towards her and his irritation at anyone else within ear-shot, causing a few to fall as collateral damage. People began to avoid him, his bad moods not worth the effort of surviving an encounter with him. Their exasperation and indignation, at being dragged into the middle of the duelling contestants, only added fodder to an already explosive developing situation.

She would drive into the side entrance at great speed, bumping and thumping over the speed bumps and screeching to a last minute halt in front of his unit. Sometimes, pulling up so close to the wall, those watching would wait, unmoving, convinced a loud crash and a tumbling wall, was imminent. Getting out of the car and slamming the door as hard as she could, she would stumble and trip her way to his door, banging on it with clenched fists. Slurring, as she loudly called out the younger man's name until, sullen faced, he would open it and take her inside, glaring at anyone who stood about innocently witnessing this particular days' performance.

The little girl, who was mostly with her on these occasions and not at school where she was meant to be, forgotten, left sitting alone in the back seat, would be rescued by one of the tenants who would get her out of the car and take her to an outside table, offering a cold drink and conversation in an attempt to distract the frightened and upset child.

This process went on for some time, slowly and predictably escalating as the weeks went by, until their original love and the innocence of it, was long forgotten. Finally, the younger man called a halt to their relationship. Telling the woman it was not working and that it was no longer a healthy environment for any of them. He had made his mind up in an instant one day, when the drunken 'two and throw,' had finally made no sense at all, anymore.

The little girl, who would now have to contend with her mothers' constant wailing and her anger over the loss of her younger mans' interest, had seen this all before, and with that same resilience of the young, did not appear to be too fazed by it all, to the surprise of the neighbours who worriedly concerned themselves over her. She was contentedly accustomed to sitting talking and playing with the residents, who all loved the little girl and her happy nature. She was well spoilt by everyone, even the most toughened souls, and she would often find a new toy left out for her to take home.

For a few weeks the dust settled and all seemed to be quiet, on the face of it. It appeared the woman had finally accepted the way things had gone. Maybe experience had won over, finally. That is, until one Saturday afternoon around three o'clock or so, and after the woman had been brooding all day in the company of a bottle of Whisky. This time, when she drove into the side entrance at great speed, bumping and thumping over the speed bumps, she hit them so hard one of the front tyres burst, the rest of the car groaning and slewing sideways from the impact of the destroyed tyre. On her way to a direct hit with the wall of the unit, she collected the heavy outdoor table with one side of the car, smashing the headlight and dinting the front end, coming to a stop with the bumper bar lying flat against the wall of the unit, the old building giving a great shudder. Bits of mortar and small pebbles coming down in a powdery shower, to rest untidily on the scratched and dinted bonnet of the old and accident worn, car.

The collision with the outdoor table saving the wall from what was sure to have been a complete catastrophe, since all of the units along that side of the driveway shared this one long, continuous wall. Everyone would have been homeless had such a thing occurred, not to even think about what the possible unexpected injuries, from such a huge wall collapsing, might have been. Only Providence, saving the day.

Speculating, on the calamity such a wall collapsing would have created, in such an eventuality, she would not have been at all surprised if the Koins still considered the units liveable. Already, there were a few internal walls which would collapse if you leant on them, the mortar long since gone. The clear view offered through into the unit next door, was a peeping Toms' delight. If the tenant had not been forewarned by others who had been caught out the hard way, and had covered their entire wall with a hanging of some kind or a strategically placed wardrobe, after giving up on the blind eye that had been turned by Mr and Mrs Koin when they had made any complaints about the troubling lack of privacy or security. Not wanting to pay for the complicated repairs needed to restore the walls, no comment had been forthcoming from them, and any objections from frightened residents worried about the nutter next door, were treated as if they simply had not been made at all.

As the woman threw open the car door and got out, barefoot and stumbling, she tripped over one of the cracks in the concrete driveway and fell heavily onto her side. A loud thump, as she whacked her head on the ground. Cursing, she sat up, her knees up to her chest, unconcerned with her skirt as it rode up her thighs displaying her underwear, the thin straps of her floral dress falling down over her shoulders towards her grazed and bleeding elbows. A long bleeding cut on her head where she had landed the bruising blow, dripping, she was lucky to still be conscious.

She sat, unmoving for a moment, then, shaking her head in an attempt to clear it. A dishevelled mess, her elbow raised as she brushed with shaky fingers, at the dirt mixing with the pouring blood that was coming from the bad gash along her underarm.

The little girl in the back seat was screaming, "Mummy, Mummy, stop it!"

People came running from everywhere, calling to each other and adding to the confusion, tripping over each other as they jockeyed for position, urgency and concern impelling them on. Some tried to help the woman up, others went to the child still sitting, screaming, on the back seat. The woman pushed them all out of the way as she staggered to her feet, her already slipping straps falling lower, the unsupported bodice displaying an exposed breast.

Spittle spraying, she screamed at them, "Bugger off. Leave me alone!" her usually friendly disposition forgotten, the vitriol evident on her twisted face.

Ignoring the car and her little girl, she staggered and stumbled, no less drunk, to the intended unit and lifted her closed fist to bang on the door. Before she could hit it, arm raised and fist still closed, the door opened and the younger man, taking her by the elbow, steered her abruptly and forcefully through the darkened void, into the privacy inside.

He looked back toward Mickie and yelled over the milling crowd, "Can you look after her, thanks?" motioning towards the still crying child. Mickie nodded his head, already getting the little girl out of the car, pushing others aside and out of his way, the singling out and the responsibility of the request, swelling his chest.

"Come on, come with me. Mummy will be alright. Come on, now," he told her, with an obvious awkwardness in having to deal with anyone this height or age.

Looking back over his shoulder toward the small crowd checking out the damage done to the car, he called to no one in particular, "Someone please take the keys out of the ignition, we don't want her to drive it again!" "Give them to me!" he added as an afterthought, now almost to the door of his own unit. In his confused way, forgetting the useless tyre stranding her there.

He sat the little girl at his outside table and told her to wait there, not to move or go anywhere, while he went inside to get her a comforting drink and some biscuits. Fumbling in his usual dithering way, unsure of how to occupy her or console her, now. A few neighbours, not wanting to get too close to the carnage or an expected participation of any forthcoming clean-up, coming to his rescue as they sat down around her, forming a protective circle.

Their welcome company offering enough of a distraction to ease her crying, even making her laugh a little half-heartedly as some of them jokingly threw orders around to those more inclined to pick up bits and pieces of the car, "Oh, you missed a bit. That's it, you lazy bludgers!" one of them yelled out, trying hard to entertain her. The little girl, tears leaving grimy tracks down her face, was calming down with the comfort offered by the others, contentedly relieved that someone else would handle her drunken mum and her impossible behaviour.

They could hear the woman screaming loudly at the younger man, the volume permitting no mistakes in the accusations she levelled at him.

"Did you fuck her too!" she yelled. "Hey? I bet you fucked all of them!" she repeated loudly, without giving pause for an answer. The younger man could be heard trying to calm her, his voice low and soothing.

The small crowd, deciding the action was over, with some having things to go and do, others just growing bored now, slowly dispersed back to their lives. All of them checking on the little girl first, offering her reassurances as they went on their way.

The loud accusations continued for an hour or so, the woman determined to have her own way about the younger mans' infidelity and his lack of loyalty. Finding it easier to blame such things than her own intolerable behaviour, and the toll it had taken on their near perfect love.

Finally, when the woman quieted, more in exhaustion than anything else, the younger man opened his door, leaning out, he called to Mickie, "Are you alright there?"

Mickie nodded his head. He had placed a colouring book in front of the little girl, and a new packet of coloured crayons that he had been saving for his sons' next rare visit.

"I've slipped her a Valium, let her sleep it off for a while," the younger man continued.

Mickie asked, "Will she be alright?" he pointed haphazardly toward the general direction of the younger man's unit, concerned curiosity sounding in his voice.

The younger man nodded his head while he confoundedly, shrugged his shoulders.

Mickie, looking down at the little girl, said, "I'll feed her and don't worry, I have the car keys, Okay?" as he distractedly motioned towards the old car, still resting against the wall.

"I'll look after it all!" he called to the younger man almost as an afterthought, as he disappeared back inside, closing the door behind himself and leaving Mickie to ponder on what to do next.

He would look after it, alright! And… the drama that was to follow.

The little girl sat outside at the old rickety table for the next few hours, colouring in and cutting out, while Mickie came and went from inside his unit, fixing her sandwiches and giving her a drink of whatever cordial he could find. Sometimes stopping to comment on her work and pointing something out to her here and there, then generally moving on, to leave her to the grand designs she was working so diligently on.

Keeping a watchful eye from his front door, his nervousness at how to handle this situation confusing him and keeping him somewhat, at bay. Having these quiet minutes to think things over, his confused mind spinning, he finally decided to hand the problem on, giving it to those who could better deal with it than he ever could.

Besides, his Christian priorities told him that no one should be allowed to put a child into such circumstances and get away with it. It was unthinkable to him, that this was such a daily event. It was as simple as that. He needed to tell on her. And the best people to tell on her to, would be those who could do something about it, and maybe save any reoccurrences into the future. Intending to get the best bang for your buck so to speak, he went for a beauty.

In the late afternoon, a Patrol Car slid quietly to a halt beside the rickety table in front of the unit. Two young Officers stepped out and walked to the open front door, calling Mickie's name as they waited. One of them, standing closer to the little girl, who was now happily tinkering with a pair of paper scissors and her cut out dolls, softly asked her how her work was progressing and what her name was. He hunkered down beside her, listening encouragingly to her tale.

By the time they had heard all the stories, and had taken the time to sit with the little girl, prompting her and gentling out what had happened that morning, it was a good two hours later and they were still in the process of deciding who the little girl should go to stay with, for the time being. Mickie continually advocated members of his Church who would be glad to look after her. Fighting hard for this outcome, knowing how the prestige of being involved in such an ugly situation and sorting it out by promoting their Church, would lift him higher in their ranks and esteem. The little girl wanted to go and stay with her older brother and his live-in girlfriend, saying, "They don't live far from here and she will be home now."

When the older brother won out, and the little girl was bundled into the back seat of the Patrol car, she waved happily to all her new friends as the Police car turned onto the Main road and sped away, to deliver her safely back into the protective arms of her own family.

A scowling Mickie, still shaking his head at being thwarted in his famousness, raised an inadvertent hand in farewell, looking more like a dismissal than a wave.

The woman, they would catch up with at a later, more sober time. Deciding it was wisest to leave her where she was, sleeping it off, they made Mickie promise not to hand her keys back to her before this, no matter what. The Department of Children's Services would be notified as an automatic, from the forwarded Police Report. Things would not go well for the woman in the floral dress, after this last and final public confrontation.

Twilight was moving into the darkness of night when there was a loud crash, as the door of the younger mans' unit flew open, slamming against the outside brick wall. The old building, shuddering from yet another impact, moaned loudly. The woman in the floral dress stormed through the door, yelling abuse at the younger man behind her, who was holding firm to one of her wrists and trying frantically to slow down her progress. Begging her to wait a moment, and to talk about it first, before doing anything else rash or stupid, that would only get her deeper into the hot water, she was already wading in.

"No! Fuck you!" the woman screamed, twisting away from him. "I'm gonna kill the mongrel bastard!" she spat out as she wrenched her wrist free from his grip, leaving reddening streaks from the scrape of his blunt nails.

Spluttering and muttering a continual barrage of swearing and threats, she half ran, half stumbled, tripping and falling, picking herself up, continuing on, all the time wrestling and writhing with the younger man, until she reached Mickie's door and began to pound on it with her closed fists.

Instead of opening the door, Mickie stood on the other side of it speaking quietly to the woman, who continued to bang on the door, the tempo not slowing.

"Open the door you fucking coward. You dog!" she declared, as if a foul taste was in her mouth. "Come on, open the door, I'm gonna flatten you, you turd!" she screeched, becoming frustrated with the unrelenting closed door in front of her, still fighting off the young mans' attempts to capture her in his grip.

Mickie, from the behind the sanctuary and safety of his door, calling back to her that her daughter was with her son now, and that she should just catch a taxi home, or go to her son's apartment. Stuttering and stammering, his efforts for clear speech aggravated further, by his deeply felt fear. She did not wait for him to finish his attempted explanations.

"Yeah, you turd," she yelled back, "What right did you have to call the Police? You fucking dog!"

The woman's crumpled, dirty dress slipping off one bruised and bloodied shoulder again, her dishevelled hair in wild array, her feet bare, and a big blue black bruise on one of her cheeks adding to the frightening effect of her contorted face. To the confused, befuddled Mickie, she was horror incarnate. His deep fear, at this imagined demon determined to get through his doorway, twisting and broiling his tightened and overworked stomach, unable to control himself, he began to retch.

Mickie stuttered and stammered, telling her firmly, "There is no way I am opening the door to you. Go away. Go home, now!"

"What about my keys? Where are my fucking keys?" she yelled, almost a whine.

The younger man, still trying to get a hold on her, or to get her to come back to his unit, begged her to stop, telling her again, "Before you end up in more trouble than you are already in." "He'll call the Police again, you know he will," he told her resolutely, "You will only make things so much worse." The younger man, still fighting for a grasp on his slithering opponent, was amazed by her strength, the adrenalin on her side.

"I want my keys!" she yelled back at him.

Mickie, getting some control over himself, his tone now a little cajoling said, "Just go home. Come back tomorrow. I can't give you the keys now. I'm not allowed to, you know that. Just go home and sleep it off. Leave it until tomorrow," his stuttering still evident, and his fear growing again with each passing moment, was on the verge of calling for reinforcements once again.

"And where is my daughter, you fucker? Hey, where's my daughter?" her voice rising again in pitch. Feeling the need to just slug him one, her persistence mounted.

"She is at your son's," Mickie answered her from the other side of the door, "I told you that, already! She's just fine, go home to her."

"You Fuuucckkeerr…!" she screamed, spit spraying the glass of the front door, still fighting off the younger mans' seeking arms.

Breaking free of the flailing arms for a moment, the woman spun around, quickly bending down she picked up a large rock from the small garden near her feet and in one swift move, slammed the rock into the glass panel of the front door, spraying shards of glass all over her and the surrounding ground and gardens. The crashing sounds echoing loudly in the quiet of the early evening. Lights flickered with the movement of drawn curtains. The younger man standing frozen nearby, his arms now immobile and still outstretched, seeking the quarry he could not quite get a hold of.

Mickie, who had ducked at the last minute, was spared the flying glass as it sailed around his lounge room, frightening him more than ever. Only his dithering processes saving him from rushing for his phone. That, and the terror of any recriminations that would follow such a move, whispering to him from the back of his mind somewhere.

"I'll call the Police if you don't just leave," he now yelled at the woman, confirming the younger mans' fears. The sincerity of this threat was clear in his attempted no-nonsense, tone. His hand already resting on the cradled phone.

The younger man, finding his ability to move again and quickly taking his opportunity, wrapped his arms tightly around the woman from behind in a bear hug. With renewed effort, fear of the repercussions encouraging him on, pinning her arms to her sides, he dragged her back from the door, making towards his own unit.

"Ouch! Ouch!" she screamed. "Fuucckk! The glass! My feet!" she tried to yell at the younger man, twisting haphazardly in his grasp as she did so.

Realising the woman was barefoot amongst all of the shattered glass shards on the ground, the younger man lifted her slightly, careful not to drop her, not losing his momentum, he continued to carry her in a bear hug towards his door, leaving a trail of dripping blood on the concrete behind them from her slashed and stained feet, the tiny shards of glass embedded deeply.

Kicking and thrashing as she went, the woman in the floral dress screamed, "Nooo....!" the whole way to the door. Her voice still ringing her protests from inside, long after the door was slammed closed behind them.

Mickie waited an hour or so before he stealthily and cautiously, slipped outside his door. A little pan and brush in his hand, he bent to sweep up the bits of glass closest to the doorstep. His obsessiveness had urged him on, the broken glass outside bothering him terribly, until he could ignore it no more. In case he had to beat a speedy retreat, he kept a watchful eye on the neighbours' door, a frightened look on his face. His hands shaking, he had difficulty keeping his grip on the little brush, dropping it to the ground a few times before finishing this important task at hand, as best he could.

The woman's raised voice, could still be heard behind the closed windows and door of her younger mans' unit. Occasionally an, "I'll get that bastard!" could be heard here and there, amongst the rest of the unfathomable tirade.

Much later, in the dead of the passing night, Mickie slipped outside again, a large envelope held tightly in one hand. Moving quietly to the younger man's unit, he stood for a moment glancing around, then taped it firmly to the door.

The large black letters saying "KEYS" standing out against the white of the envelope, could be seen easily in the darkness.

THE TRANSIT CENTRE

It had been a slow, easy morning, full of moments of reflection as she packed her belongings into her duffel bag. The small pile of things to give to a few favoured tenants growing gradually, as she had brutally cut away the unneeded from the needed.

She looked around the unit that had been her home, and her sanctuary from the chaotic madness outside the door, for the last eighteen months or so, feeling a strange kind of attachment that only time spent, can give. At the tattered, threadbare curtains gently lifting back and forth with the familiar morning sea breeze. At the torn and patchy carpet covering most of the floor. At the sad and generally unusable ancient things, like the old television and fridge which had probably been here, in the same spot, for decades now, imagining the things they had seen over all of that time. Even the musty smell, now a familiar companion, raised warm and melancholy feelings, the kind that comes with welcome goodbyes.

She stood, looking back on her time here and closing the book on what was now behind her, before she could turn to look at the road ahead. She had to admit, her excitement at the unknown of what was ahead of her, made this ritual pleasant and soothing, but also somehow exhilarating. As well as it being her spiritualistic form of closure and cleansing, a way of honouring all and who, that had been part of that short time in her life, but taking none of it with her into the purity and potential of what was to come.

She would not tell anyone she was leaving. She would put her little piles of give-aways at the doors of those receiving, with a little note wishing them well for their future lives, but that was all. She knew she would never see any of them again, and that was as it should be. Her going, would be as ambiguous and silent as her stay here, a burden to none and a private journey, all of her own.

With a sigh, she shoved the last of what she was taking with her into her duffel bag.

The unit, now cleaned and tidied, could be put away and forgotten, leaving her time to take a walk around the small Town. To say goodbye to the lovely beaches, to look one last time at the Casino like Clubs, the expensive cars resting, waiting, in their allotted carparks for loud and lusty celebrating owners to come and collect them. To listen to the noises of the partying holiday-makers coming from the open doorways of the pubs, clubs and cafes, their merriment contagious to any surrounding onlookers. The occasional brawling of enthusiastic young men, and mostly ignored, amid the drunken gaiety of other revellers, their spirits undaunted. The smell of money was everywhere, both spent and sought. She would miss the rush and bustle. Almost.

Most of all, she would miss the beaches. The long walks on golden, white beaches, the sound of the ocean in the quiet of the night, the smell of salt always in the air, the screeches of the sea gulls harassing passers-by for thrown titbits. But she would remember, and that was good enough.

She sat for a while looking out to sea, the great modern apartment blocks at her back, watching the huge container ships following their only allowed, designated path along the Coastline. This had always been her most favourite of pastimes and chosen now, to be her last look at the beautiful Coastline she had called home, for so little a time. The massive ships, bouncing and bobbing, seemingly so alarmingly close to the shore, then quickly steaming out of sight, one after another.

As if on cue, a homeless man stumbled past on the concrete pathway in front of her. She wondered momentarily, if it was the same man she had seen when she had first arrived. She hoped it was, but somehow, she knew it was not. She watched him, almost affectionately, until he turned a corner and was gone, forever, from her sight.

Her alarm had been set for 3.30 a.m. but she had not really slept anyway, only dozing here and there. She did not mind her wakefulness, though. She loved those silent times of night, when, if you applied enough imagination to the task, you could be reminded of what it must have been like when it was a quiet, sleepy fishing Village. A time not so far distant, as the hectic, modern, industrious developments might now suggest.

Rousing herself, she headed for the shower, knowing she had only an hour or so, before her bus would leave the Transit Centre on its' way to the nearest inland Railway Station, and the continued journeys that began there.

Her duffel bag waited by the front door. She had already placed her little parcels outside of the very few doors of their new homes, so it was only a matter of getting dressed and heading out the door. Her times for contemplation was over, only the road ahead in sight. Excited now, the day ahead beckoned her, and she had always loved to see the countryside passing by, taking her on her way to new horizons. She had said all the unspoken farewells she wanted to, so she got about her business now, with a relaxed ease and pace.

Taking her final brief look around the intimate and comforting unit, she turned the light out, quietly closing the door with a small click behind her, for the last time. She made her way up the main driveway, toward the little Office. The crunching of the gravel under her feet as she made her way along, sounding louder to her ears in the surrounding complete silence, briefly wondering if any of the neighbours were up and about in their darkened world, and able to hear this racket, also. Would they glance outside, to see who it was disturbing their private place.

Stopping only long enough to put her unit keys in an envelope marked "Mr and Mrs Koin," and to place it inside the communal mailbox in the wall, she hurried on her way. Hurrying, not because she was late but because she wanted a moment, a last look back, when she made the top of the hill ahead of her. Reaching the lip of the main driveway, she paused for a moment to look down at the great sign that rested on the ground, its' lengthy bulk leaning back against the long hedgerow. Someone had recorded their own irritation for all to see, passing sentence on the Complex in sloppy white dripping paint, the words handwritten, small one moment and large the next, beneath the large white printed 'KOINS MOTEL,' was their perfectly centred '(the last resort).' She sighed, but it also made her smile.

Arriving at the slight rise at the top of the main road before it dipped back down towards the beach, putting her duffel bag on the ground, she stopped and turned to take a slow and final look over the sleeping Complex, now appearing so benign in its' slumber. Trying hard now, to see it as she had that first time, without any familiarity clouding her view or changing her perspective, her memory taking her back to a time when it had appeared so deserted, a home only for the cats, who had watched her passage from under the bushes protecting them from this intruder.

She had learnt, that the vicious nature of the people who lived here, had not been accorded to only those who knew no better, or whose struggles in life had bestowed them with exhaustion of any love for those around them. She knew now, that the same viciousness was held close and practised well by those who had much to be thankful for in their abundant lives, also. That human beings were still the best commodity of all, one way or another.

She looked down at the great black giant, sleeping so peacefully, below her. It was still that heavy darkness of just before the dawns' growing light, which would soon rise behind her, over the blue green ocean. The air was moist with the night dew. She took in a deep breath, feeling the invigorating slight wetness on her skin. The fronds of the tall Palm trees standing sentinels along the lower driveway, gently moved when caught by the sea breeze. Their huge knuckled trunks were long black slashes against a sky still full of stars. A perfect complement, to the sleeping giant they accompanied.

She picked her duffel bag up and hanging it over her shoulder, she took one last look around. Pushing away the feelings of sadness for those who still found shelter there, before she turned back to the journey before her, and the as yet, unfulfilled day to come .

On time, the big Coach squeaked and wheezed its' way into the waiting bay. Coming to an abrupt and sudden halt, the doors clapped noisily open.

The handful of people in the Transit Centre at this time of the morning, were made up mainly of early shift workers. Taking no notice of each other, on their own habitual journeys, they moved toward their buses, some yawning, none were smiling. The whole scene contradicted the crowded, jostling, busyness, the Centre would be in a few hours' time.

She let everyone who was lining up for her bus, push amongst each other as they sought unthinkingly, impatiently, to get themselves onto the bus and safely on their way.

She waited, the last one to board. Smiling broadly, she said, "Good Morning" to the silent bus driver as he flipped the doors closed behind her.

THE END

ABOUT THE AUTHOR

D. O'Brien is a mother of four, and grandmother of five grandchildren. She has a College Certificate in Business and has spent most her working life self-employed. In her early career, she was employed for thirteen years at one of the major Metropolitan News Papers, first of all working for Fairfax and then later, Murdoch.

After this time, she went on to a few brief incarnations, such as renovating and restoring then selling on, original Queenslanders. This, leading her to spend a few years as a Real Estate Consultant in one of the prettiest areas of Australia. Finally, using her knowledge of Marketing and Business Management, she went on to establish and manage her own Importing/Wholesale Business for fifteen years until she retired.

She now lives a quiet life full of grandchildren, gardening and writing.

Printed in Australia
AUOC02n0948080616
276494AU00003B/3/P